Cool, Calm, and Respected

8 Leadership Concepts for Work and Home

What Management Taught Me About Parenting
- and Vice Versa

Diane Chang

Cool, Calm, and Respected: 8 Leadership Concepts
for Work and Home

ISBN: 978-1-52-113989-9

This book is dedicated to Malcolm,
Talisa, and Brandon
- My husband and children who make me proud every
day -

It is a tribute to "Popo"
- My beautiful and amazing grandmother who passed
away at the age of 101 years while this book was
going into publication –

Table of Contents

Introduction

On occasion, my husband and I have been told that we are "cool" parents. We have surmised that we are seen as cool not because we're permissive to the point of negligence, or because we're more of a friend than a parent; instead, we're the kind of cool that avoids drama in our interactions with our children, that encourages communication and openness, and above all, that resolves conflict without resorting to ultimatums and the "because I said so" fallback.

Our coolness factor was upped when, much to the surprise of our friends, we decided to turn our comfortable suburban lives in sunny Southern California upside down and move to New York City. Our family and friends told us they envied our courage to take a leap of faith and carve out a whole new life late in our careers. It felt easier to tell people that our main motivation was to be closer to our children who had moved to the East Coast after attending college there. But, truth be told, we were somewhat envious of the new adventures they were having and thought it was time for one of our own. So, we sold our spacious 4-bedroom home and everything we owned—except for whatever we managed to fit into two 5x7x8 U-Haul containers and our minivan—and made our way to the Big Apple via a two-week road trip.

It was an indescribable thrill for us to arrive in Manhattan at night to the voice of Alicia Keys belting out *New York.*[1] I have goose bumps all over again as I write this and remember those first unforgettable moments. We were feeling brand new, just as the song said we would. Up until then, I'd worked in the Information Technology field for over 25 years. I started my career in Johannesburg, South Africa, as a developer for a software development and consulting company. After immigrating to North America I worked for a related company as a developer, analyst, and pre- and post-sales software engineer. When the travel expectations became more than I could manage with a young family, I found a job with a privately held investment management organization based out of Los Angeles, California. In the sixteen years I worked there, I had multiple exciting roles that included managing large teams and multi-million, multi-year development projects.

As part of our move, I quit this great job with an excellent company that I thought I would retire from. It was challenging at times, but I had many opportunities to grow and learn alongside talented colleagues. Some of them have become lifelong friends who continue to shape my leadership thinking. During my two-months notice period, it was heartwarming that many people stopped by my office to wish me well. While they were excited for me, what really struck me was the sadness expressed at the loss of a senior manager who they believed embodied the core values that were the foundation of a positive corporate culture. They were proud of not only what we accomplished together, but also of how we did it. We worked collaboratively, respected and trusted each other, and had a lot of fun. Some, including myself, however, felt that the actions of certain leaders were no longer aligned with the core values that we held so dearly, and the shift had become a demotivating distraction.

It was humbling to learn that a few coworkers thought I was a pretty "cool" manager too. It's easy to become hotheaded under stress, especially if you have a tendency towards blaming rather than solving. I recall an instance when I first took on responsibility for our new Customer Relationship Management application. We had a critical system outage that required a coordinated investigation by multiple technical teams. On the cross-team triage call, I calmly asked questions about what we were observing, and solicited ideas from each team representative to determine appropriate next steps. We ended the call after finalizing an action plan and agreeing to a follow-up call an hour later. Within seconds of hanging up, my phone rang. It was an engineer from another team who wanted to let me know how refreshing it was that my priority was to focus the group on solving the issue, without trying to find someone to blame and publicly chastise. Because there was no yelling, he was in a better position, mentally and emotionally, to determine the root cause, and he thanked me. As I reflected on his words, it dawned on me that I had never personally been yelled at for mistakes I had made. I was simply mirroring how my parents and managers had treated me and what I observed in other respected leaders.

Over my decades-long career, I've been exposed to many leadership styles. And I've often wondered what "bad" bosses were like as parents. Did they spread toxicity at home too? Or did they switch their tone on the commute home? If they were rigid at work, were they stricter parents? Were their personality traits amplified or subdued depending on their environment or their audience? On the flip side, I wondered if fantastic parents were also great leaders at work. Maybe they weren't reaching their full potential because they didn't feel as confident at work, or because they didn't have a designated leadership title.

I decided to write this book when I realized that the way I approached management had many parallels to the way my husband and I approached parenting. While there are thousands of tomes on leadership, management, and parenting, this book shows how we can transfer our skills and experience from the office to the home and vice versa.

This is not to say that employees should be treated like kids in the workplace. Rather, it's about recognizing that the roles we have as leaders at work and in our families both require a shared set of competencies, a consistent persona, and the same foundation of core values.

Our persona is the way we behave and present ourselves to others that causes them to perceive us in a certain way. While we can certainly draw boundaries between our private and professional lives, having vastly different personal and private personas can reduce our ability to be authentic leaders and to gain universal respect and trust.

It has been said that to truly gauge a person's character, you should observe how they interact with someone who can offer them no benefit. I believe that we should treat colleagues, family, friends and strangers alike with dignity and respect at all times, and that we should earn their trust and respect while being true to who we are. I believe that we can and should help each other more than we realize, and that we need to look beyond our fears if we want to live without regrets. Most importantly, I believe that warm-hearted, compassionate, and nurturing leaders are necessary to create environments in which others can thrive.

It's difficult to bring together a multidisciplinary team of talented individuals; it's more difficult to keep them actively engaged. Actively engaged employees can have an impact on the bottom line and are more likely to innovate. You may not lose them physically to a different team or organization, but losing them mentally might be worse for everyone in the long run. When it comes to your family and close friends, even the slightest misunderstanding can sever or erode a once mutually respectful relationship.

I am passionate about improving corporate culture and society. It's a reason why I decided to become a professional coach. I want to be a better leader and help others do the same for their families and teams.

For this book, I've drawn upon my experience as a manager, employee, colleague, mentor, mentee, coach, student, spouse, parent, daughter, granddaughter, sibling, niece, cousin, aunt, and friend. The principles I share in each of the eight leadership concepts have helped me work through my own challenges and have helped me coach others to work through theirs.

The book is designed to be brief, while providing enough information about each concept to illustrate the underlying principle and the way in which it applies at work and at home. I've listed some helpful tips and examples. While I haven't included parallel examples for every concept, the idea is that you'll make the connections and translate them to your own personal and professional situations, whatever they may be. And while the way in which we show up as leaders can have serious ramifications, my wish is that you will enjoy some of the light-hearted angles.

As Alicia Keys says in the official music video. "I want to play this for you different than you ever heard before."

Perhaps you too will find that…

To be "cool" you really have to be "warm."

To be calm takes and makes positive energy.

To be respected by those you care about simply takes being respectful to others and yourself.

"Respect is how you treat everyone, not just those you want to impress."
- Richard Branson

Chapter 1
Helicopters and
Humvees®

© Diane Chang Coaching

Unexpectedly, the steady drone of the helicopter rotors has a calming effect on you. It's a beautiful sunny day and you can see the magnificent aerial view of tropical rivers snaking through a lush emerald rainforest. As you swoop towards the ocean, the rivers become waterfalls that spill over cliffs, creating clouds of mist. You trace the water as it gathers into ponds and lakes, eventually emptying into pristine beaches.

A few hours later you're in a Humvee, bumping around the forest floor at night, your shirt sticky with sweat. With help from the guide and huge spotlights, you see a herd of bearded pigs snuffling in the undergrowth. Suddenly, they flee at the sharp warning bark of a macaque. Perhaps a jaguar is stalking them. The driver cuts all power and you gasp at the luminous fungi, glowing like earthbound jellyfish. All the while, the fragrant orchids and rotting fruit on the forest floor assail your nostrils.

Back in the hotel lounge, sipping a mojito, you're pleased with your decision to splurge on both tours. The dense foliage hid a myriad of wonders from the aerial view. But from the ground, you couldn't have fully appreciated the vast extent of the rainforest - how the rivers shaped the landscape, and even the climate. By foregoing a coin toss, you gained two entirely different perspectives.

Helicopters and Humvees®

Many years ago at a leadership offsite, surrounded by multiple diagrams on flipcharts, I noticed that most of us were becoming increasingly frustrated at our inability to agree on how to restructure our teams. I was a relatively new manager at the time, and along with my peers, could not understand why those to whom we reported were proposing an organization structure that seemed less than optimal. Similarly, our senior leaders were perplexed by our reluctance to get behind the idea.

An image popped into my head. I saw our senior managers up in helicopters radioing down instructions to us, while we were moving supplies through the dense forest in our Humvees (High Mobility Multipurpose Wheeled Vehicle). It seemed as though they were asking us to cross the river at the narrowest and seemingly easiest spot, in spite of how treacherous that rocky section was. Our proposal to cross further downstream at a wider, calmer section seemed time-consuming and unnecessary to them. They obviously did not want us to risk our lives, but it didn't seem that way to us at the time. There was clearly a disconnect and we left the offsite without consensus, amid some grumbling and head scratching. Even though we were communicating, we could not see each other's perspective.

Through a series of follow-up meetings, we all happily agreed on a hybrid of the options from the offsite. However, we could only do that after we all gained more insight into the implications of various structures from both the strategic and operational perspectives. Even if we had selected the original option proposed by our leaders, it would have been easier for us to get behind it after learning the rationale upon which it was based. Had we been forced to implement their proposal immediately after the offsite, the grumbling would probably have gotten louder and some of us might have developed a "why bother" attitude that lingered for years, feeling our input was not considered or respected. I also started to wonder whether I was engaging and supporting my own team in a way that would earn their respect.

It occurred to me that "Helicopters and Humvees" provide distinct yet complementary views of the same environment. They each have highly specialized capabilities that are best for different situations—yet we don't always embrace these benefits in our daily lives.

From a helicopter you have a view far into the distance, over mountains and trees, across land and water. You can see how the terrain changes in different parts of the rainforest and which areas might be accessible by air, land or water. Besides providing an aerial view, a helicopter is extremely versatile. It can hover, manage vertical takeoffs and landings, and offer forward, backward, and lateral movement. Very often helicopters are called in to support ground operations or used as a swift means of transport when no other alternative is available.

On the other hand, the four-wheel drive Humvee provides an on-the-ground view. It can travel over inhospitable terrain to places inaccessible by a helicopter. It can ford depths of up to five feet of water and carry heavy equipment. From its vantage point, you can identify blocked routes and obstacles that render certain paths impassable.

In many ways, the helicopter view is that of upper management or anyone who manages others. We expect executives and senior managers to have a vision, provide direction, and develop the broader strategies for their organizations based on this perspective. They're also there to provide resources and remove roadblocks for their teams to accomplish the desired goal.

This is also the view of parents, who have a role in planning for their family's future. They make decisions for the whole family on where to live, go to school, take vacations, and how to pay for it all. Grandparents might be called on to lend their child rearing experience for babysitting. Or, they may take on a mentorship role.

The Humvee is typically the view from which middle management and team members operate. They are intimately acquainted with the inner workings of an organization (and we all know that "the devil is in the details") and have a better sense of the day-to-day challenges and opportunities.

In the family setting, it is the children who are in the Humvee. They are the ones making their way through life, navigating obstacles, learning about the limits and possibilities of their own paths, and looking to their parents for guidance and direction. As old as we are, our parents still see us as their kids.

Note:

This is not to say that employees should be treated like children in the workplace. This is about recognizing that the roles we have at work and within our families provide us with both the helicopter and Humvee perspectives.

Enthuse both views

At different times in our professional and personal lives we're getting either the helicopter *or* the Humvee view, depending on our role as parent, child, executive, manager, or individual contributor. When you're reporting to someone and also have others reporting to you, you're rapidly switching between the Humvee and the helicopter views. That's why middle management can be challenging at times. This is especially true when you feel conflicted between the expectations of you in your Humvee role and what you value for your team when you're in your helicopter role.

Irrespective of our role at a given time, we have the choice to use our mode of transport to either create distance or come together frequently. By choosing the latter, we can get a better appreciation of what both the helicopter *and* Humvee offer.

Tap into them

Don't waste the potential or versatility of both helicopters and Humvees to support your family or team. Tap into the unique vantage points of your entire team or family.

Connect them

While some distance between the helicopters and Humvees is required for them to effectively perform in their space, make every effort to keep them healthily and collaboratively connected.

Experience them

You can imagine and appreciate what it's like to be in a helicopter or Humvee, but experiencing them firsthand provides invaluable and memorable insight.

"The more you know, the more you know you don't know."

- Aristotle

Attend to the other view

Appreciate, and whenever possible, experience life from the other side. Although you don't have to be a tennis player to recognize the talent of Roger Federer, it's only after you've hit a ball yourself that you understand how much skill and practice it takes to hit those incredible shots with such grace and accuracy.

Take advantage of the strengths of both helicopters and Humvees irrespective of your primary role in the workplace or home. If we develop strategies and plans without taking into account pertinent information from our teams and families, there will be gaps in the plan or challenges in the implementation. An uninformed decision is rarely a good one. In situations when helicopter decisions must be made without consulting others, share the rationale for the decision to reduce the risk of others making incorrect assumptions that could create

unwanted distance and distrust. To create sound
Humvee implementation plans, those on the ground
must understand the bigger picture.

Irrespective of your role, find ways to connect the
view in meaningful ways. Frequently interacting in
deliberate and positive ways helps to build mutual
respect and trust.

From the helicopter role

When you're acting as a manager or parent you're
flying high in the helicopter.

- *Take a Humvee ride*

   Those in helicopters run the risk of flying so
   high, that they become detached from everyday
   realities. Don't keep your head in the clouds
   unless you want to be seen as elitist and aloof.

   While management retreats and distance are
   necessary to reflect, re-plan, and rejuvenate,
   executives and senior managers shouldn't lose
   sight of the daily challenges others are facing.
   Most senior executives are fortunate to have
   experienced the Humvee view as they rose
   through the ranks. However, they run the risk of
   losing sight of this perspective or of not realizing
   that job functions have changed since they had a
   Humvee role. Leaders in helicopters must take a
   ride in the Humvee periodically and spend
   quality time with their teams. The goal isn't for
   them to do the work on the ground, but to
   actively engage and appreciate the real
   challenges at that level. In doing so, they can
   more readily assist in removing roadblocks and

providing the necessary resources for their teams to get the job done. Parents also run the risk of becoming out of touch with each generation's new growing pains. Growing up today is very different from growing up a few decades ago. Each generation has an ever-changing set of opportunities, struggles, and social norms. With technological advances and global access to social media and information, it makes it paradoxically harder and easier for parents to keep up with what their children are dealing with. Parents who are mindful of bridging the generation gap can provide guidance and make decisions in a more informed manner. When they try to experience life in the same way as their children, it shows their children that they are willing to see things in a different way to their potentially institutionalized view, and it makes them more approachable and relatable. Parents—wanting the best for their children, but perhaps stuck in the mindset of a bygone age—may insist on their offspring pursuing a career in medicine or finance, since that was their ideal path to upward mobility. There are many more options available today that young adults might find more personally rewarding. In ten years from now, jobs will exist that we haven't even thought of yet. For instance, who knew in the 60's and 70's that someone could be a social media manager, or a nanotechnology engineer?

- *Don't be a helicopter parent*
  There is also risk in helicopters flying too low. Helicopters that fly too low create turbulence on the ground, obscuring vision by whipping up dust, and drowning out conversation with their noisy proximity.

  Helicopter parents constantly hover over their children. They interfere with and become overinvolved in their children's lives. They are overprotective and do tasks their children are physically, emotionally, and mentally capable of doing on their own. This applies when their child is a toddler and continues all the way to adulthood. Who has not heard tales of a mother who continues to give her daughter a wake up call—while she is three thousand miles away in college, or the parent who accompanies their child to their first job interview?

  These parents don't allow their children to face and overcome their own challenges, to learn through their mistakes, and to take pride in their own accomplishments. As a result, the child's development and coping skills are stunted and they may not develop the self-confidence to cope with inevitable setbacks. Parents must find ways to stay engaged without hovering, even if it means having to watch their children struggle and fail, in order to learn valuable life lessons.

  Similarly, helicopter managers have a tendency to micromanage their teams and their projects. Micromanagers do not delegate well and pay excessive attention to small, procedural details that their teams can handle on their own.

In doing so, they do not create an environment where employees feel trusted and empowered, leading to disengagement and resentment. They also run the risk of being so bogged down in the details that they lose sight of the bigger picture and of the overall objectives. They have less time to devote to formulating the strategic direction for the long-term success and relevance of the team.

- *Extend an invitation for a helicopter ride*

  People in helicopter roles can be intimidating, whether or not they mean to be. It doesn't need to be lonely at the top. Determine when it's appropriate to disclose to your teams and families what you face in your role.

  At work, your teams probably have a better idea of what is practical because they understand the nuances of the situation. They are also specialists in their field who know what equipment and skill sets are needed to execute the plan and realize the vision. Many of them can even develop part of the vision as they prepare for a helicopter role in the future.

  At home, your family might better understand why you made certain decisions on their behalf. If they invented reasons about your rationale, incorrect assumptions they made may have undesired long-term consequences in the way they think about you or themselves.

  How many times have you heard "because I said so!" in a response to your question about a decision? You probably felt that it was an unsatisfying and unproductive, if not cowardly answer. If you were the one giving the response (as a manager or as a parent), you undoubtedly realized it was a cop out even as you were saying it. Maybe it's because you had no time to explain your reasoning. Perhaps you were unsure of yourself.

What's certain is that it was a lost opportunity to build mutual understanding and respect. As the decision-maker, even if you believe the decision is yours alone to make, it's worth taking the time and effort to share your thought process – and to allow others to share theirs.

Inviting others to take a ride in the helicopter periodically will give them a better appreciation of the bigger picture, and more importantly, they might be able to help solve a problem once they see both views.

- *Provide a parachute*
  When someone has taken the time and effort to share an idea or raise an issue, be mindful of how you respond. Not everyone will see eye-to-eye on all topics. When there is a disagreement, let the individual know respectfully and take the appropriate course of action. Don't push them out of the helicopter without a parachute. Not only will this discourage others from taking a ride, but it will also result in long-term damage to a relationship and it could be viewed as victimization if done repeatedly.

An extreme example is parents who disown their children, or managers who fire those who don't always agree with them. While a helicopter is informally known as a "chopper," chopping the heads off those who aren't "yes-men" is not the answer. Instead, use disagreements as an opportunity to really understand the information discussed, to establish rapport, and to build a relationship. If a point of view is contradictory to yours, you might even be persuaded to change yours for a better outcome. Even if you can't be persuaded, express gratitude to the individual for raising the topic, and help them better understand your viewpoint. Imagine that you were in their position and think about how you would want to be treated. Also remember that others are observing how you treat those who express an opinion different to yours.

• *Leverage your helicopter's unique abilities*

An air ambulance is often used for emergency medical assistance when a land vehicle can't easily reach or transport a patient. Law enforcement and military forces use helicopters, in conjunction with ground operations, to conduct tasks that can't be fully executed from the ground only. In both work and family situations, recognize when you are uniquely equipped to directly contribute to the team and family goals.

As a manager, use your influence and skills to pave the way for your teams by providing clear direction, making timely decisions, hiring additional resources, and providing the necessary training and equipment.

As a parent, be mindful of when you are uniquely equipped to keep lifting and supporting your family members. Use your life experience and relationships to expose them to new skills and to a broader perspective when they are mired in their limited view. This can range from providing transport to their daily activities to helping them to deal with physical and emotional growing pains.

- **Drop ship supplies**

  While we want our teams and families to be resourceful and figure things out for themselves as much as possible, there will always be times when "help from above" is needed. Think about *The Hunger Games* where just the right solutions were parachuted down to the competitors in times of need. While the mentors sent packages that were lifesavers, there were situations where the competitors still had to figure out what the mentors intended them to do with the gifts. I once heard that you give your children enough money to do something, but not enough to do nothing. Know when help is needed and be there for those who depend on you.

- **Move them quickly to a better place**

  When ground transport is too slow or impossible due to congestion, rough terrain, or unfavorable conditions, helicopters are used to quickly move people or equipment. They are also used for transport to remote sites and for rescue efforts.

As a manager, when you realize a team member is unhappy or mismatched in their current role, or when you recognize they have greater potential in another role or department, help them get to where they need to be, even if it means losing a talented person. Employees are assets that can contribute and develop across the entire organization. Their success is enhanced if they can perform to their strengths, which in turn, enhances the success of the company.

As a parent, when your child expresses that they are no longer interested in particular extramural activity, explore why and determine if they would be happier doing something else. If they find mid-way through college that what they thought they wanted at age 17 is not something they want to dedicate the next 20 or 40 years of their lives to, work with them to find something they might enjoy more. If it's something outside your area of expertise, work with them to find someone else who can better advise them.

In my second year of medical school in South Africa, I realized that although I had the potential to become a good doctor, I wasn't enjoying what I was doing. Given the sacrifices my mother had made to get me this far, she could have forced me to continue. Instead, she allowed me to take some time to figure out what I wanted to do. She and my aunt both gave me jobs until I decided to get into computer programming. I have never regretted that decision given the support I had. My husband, daughter, and son are all now in careers that are not directly related to their degrees, and we all support each other in our choices.

From the Humvee role

In addition to having a helicopter role as a manager or parent, you could also have a Humvee role. When you're reporting to someone or interacting with your parents or grandparents, you are on the ground in the Humvee.

- *Request a helicopter ride*

  If you've been invited for a helicopter ride, accept it. If you haven't, request one. Humvee drivers also need to see the world from the helicopter perspective.

  When flying in the helicopter, use that time to learn what a day-in-the-life looks like for those in helicopter roles. Learn more about their responsibilities and some of the challenges they face. Seemingly senseless management or parental decisions might not be perceived that way after you've taken a few rides in the helicopter.

  At work, before meeting with those in helicopter roles, solicit questions from your peers and team so that you can make the most out of what might be a rare opportunity. Ask executive and senior leadership about their strategic vision and how they see it benefitting the organization, its clients, and its employees.

Afterwards, reflect on what you learned and determine what's appropriate to share with others on the ground. Think about when you might want to ask about scheduling another ride in the future.

At home, engage in conversations with your parents and grandparents about their life's journey. You'd be surprised at how much you didn't know about how they became the people they are today. You'll also get some insight into how they developed their parenting styles. Ask about what they did or do to earn a living. Learn about how they spend their days at work and whom they interact with.

- *Tour the rough roads*

  When the helicopter travelers come down for a ride in the Humvee, don't just take them on the paved roads where it is smooth and comfortable. This is a chance to expose them to the day-to-day issues you face in the bumpiest terrains so they can experience or better appreciate what you are going through.

  In fact, the Humvee was designed primarily for personal and light cargo transport behind front lines. When it also started to serve as a front line urban combat vehicle, soldiers and marines often improvised by using scrap materials for extra armor. This made the vehicles heavier and reduced their speed, maneuverability, and lifespan. Without senior executives having this knowledge about the challenges Humvee riders were facing, armor kits would not have been installed. While Humvees are still vulnerable to attack, they are better adapted now to function in low intensity combat situations.

Don't fear that sharing your challenges will reflect negatively on you and your team, or that your parents will judge you harshly for not being able to overcome obstacles on your own. Your intent is not to complain, but to inform and to request guidance and support that only they can provide.

- *Don't let them drive*

    When managers or parents are touring with you on the ground, don't let them drive, except for a brief spin. Make them aware of how they can help in providing the resources needed to get something done. However, do not see this as an opportunity for them to do your job or your chores for you. They are there to listen, understand, and guide. They themselves may be tempted to get back into their prior roles, so help them recognize that they need to get back into that helicopter and function in their own roles so that you can continue to grow in yours.

- *Manage helicopter parents*

    As mentioned before, helicopter parents can be overbearing and stifling. If you find yourself in the position of having a helicopter parent or manager, do your best to minimize this tendency in them. While it might not be easy at first, learning how to "manage up" could improve your situation.

A micro-manager is usually not confident in the ability of their team to work independently to deliver the level of expected results. Communicate to them your understanding of the expectations of your role and deliverables, and demonstrate that you are capable of doing your job. Give them a date for when you'll be checking in with them to provide a progress update. This way they have some assurance that they will be kept in the loop and over time, they may learn how to let go.

A helicopter parent usually feels that they need to direct every move their children make. They are constantly checking on their children and lack confidence in their children's ability to cope independently. As someone in a Humvee role, show your parents that you are capable of leading a life of your own by simply doing so responsibly. Proactively check in with them if they have the tendency to worry.

- *Give them something to take back up*

  Unless you want to see each trip down as "the aliens have landed," use this opportunity to bridge the gap and to keep the communication channels open. We all need to keep learning to stay current and be relevant in an ever-changing world. Don't let the helicopter riders be stuck in a world familiar to them at the time they had a similar role to yours. Help them understand the new definition of a role that might be evolving along with the technologies that support or enhance the role.

A sense of pride might stop those in more senior roles from asking for help. However, I am constantly appreciative when our children point things out to us or advise us without solicitation. They do it in a respectful manner and they genuinely have our interests at heart when they guide us on social media, technology advances, and family matters. They also enrich our cultural experiences by exposing us to new movies, music, books, events, and attitudes.

"We need people in our lives with whom we can be as open as possible. To have real conversations with people may seem like such a simple, obvious suggestion, but it involves courage and risk."

- Thomas Moore

Key Principle and Action

Maximize and share your vantage point
The most effective visions, strategies, decisions, plans, and outcomes are usually attained when both the helicopter and the Humvee perspective are taken into account and integrated. Frequently interacting in deliberate and positive ways helps to build mutual respect and trust.

- In the multiple roles you have, make the most of what you are equipped to offer from your helicopter or Humvee vantage point to support your family or team.

- Encourage and create opportunities to work collaboratively.

- Appreciate, or whenever possible, experience it from the other side.

Chapter 2
Elephant Matriarchs and Tiger Moms

*In "Tomorrowland," the thirteenth and final episode of season 4 of **Mad Men**, there's a scene that highlights a very different approach to parenting.*

Don (Jon Hamm) takes his children, Sally (Kiernan Shipka) and Bobby (Jared Gilmore), on vacation to California. He brings his secretary, Megan (Jessica Pare), along to babysit. There's a scene in a diner where the children, are arguing. Sally shouts "Shut up!" to Bobby, and accidentally spills her milkshake all over the table.

*Don is annoyed and sarcastically utters "Great!"
as he looks for a server to clean the mess. In a calm
and friendly voice, Megan says, "Don't be upset, it's
just a milkshake," while reaching for some napkins to
wipe the spill. Don, Sally, and Bobby are visibly
stunned into silence at her response, before Don
(uncharacteristically) starts helping Megan.*

*The reason they are speechless is because had
this happened with the children's mom, Betty
(January Jones), it would have been a completely
different scene. Betty would have reprimanded and
belittled them in her typical cold, impatient manner.
And, if they were at home, she would most likely also
have sent them to their room with some form of
punishment.*

*While it may be pointless to cry over spilt milk, it
creates a toxic and unproductive situation when we
yell over spilled milkshake.*

Elephant Matriarchs and Tiger Moms

The leadership styles associated with elephant
matriarchs and tiger moms are very different. The
former is democratic and nurturing, while the latter is
authoritarian and punitive.

I believe that while different situations call for us
to select from leadership styles that range from
autocratic to laissez-faire, we tend to adopt a primary
style. I also believe that a style that is compassionate
and encouraging is far more effective in the long term

than one that is consistently demanding and controlling. Think about yourself on the receiving end of each style. Which would you prefer?

About Elephant Matriarchs

The elephant matriarch, or female leader, is usually the oldest and largest adult female member of the family. Through her research, Ethologist/Conservationist Joyce Poole believes that successful matriarchs are not self-appointed leaders.[2] They are leaders because members of their family respect them, and they are respected because they have proven over the years that they can be trusted to make wise decisions in times of crisis.

A successful matriarch needs to be both genetically and socially well connected to all members of her family. She must use her social skills to show compassion and care toward all members of her extended family, not just her own sons and daughters. She must prove to the others that she is worthy of being their leader. She does this by her display of courage and wisdom in times of crisis, by her enviable memory of places and individuals in tough or dangerous times, by her intricate use of tactics in socially difficult situations, and through her excellent social skills to regularly and consistently build, maintain and reinforce the close bonds within her family.

About Tiger Moms

The term "Tiger Mother" refers to a strict mother who demands academic perfection of her children above all else. With the best of intentions, yet not always with the best outcomes, she unrelentingly pushes her children to attain the highest level of scholastic achievement in multiple areas. Many times this comes at the sacrifice of the child's social, physical, psychological, and emotional well-being. This parenting style is often attributed to families of East, South, and Southeast Asian descent. It isn't so much an attribute of an ethnicity, but of a philosophy of expecting the best, and nothing less, from your children. The rationale of parents who adopt this outlook is that stellar academic achievement will increase their child's chances of getting accepted into the best colleges, which in turn, will increase their chances of being successful in life. In this context, success is defined in terms of social prestige, a "worthy" career choice, and financial gain. Anything less than an "A" grade is frowned upon. In fact, there's a *Fresh Off the Boat* episode where the "B-minus" grade of the family restaurant is referred to as a "Chinese F!"

This level of achievement is expected in the classroom, in science fairs, in sports, and in classical music, and requires rigorous preparation and effort on the part of their children. The tiger mom sees her role as mapping out, demanding, enforcing, and supporting this journey. To this end, she dedicates much, if not all, of her time to raising her children. She meticulously plans and monitors their schedules and output, often sacrificing her own personal needs.

"Management is about arranging and telling.
Leadership is about nurturing and enhancing."

- Tom Peters

Model the waddle

The leadership style that we adopt at work and home is a personal choice, but we can learn a lot from elephant matriarchs and tiger moms, irrespective of our gender. From tiger moms we see the benefits of diligence and resilience, but my personal inclination is to more closely model the waddle (or more accurately, the lumber) of the elephant matriarch.

Lead yourself

To be a respected leader, take responsibility for your own actions and behavior, especially when under stress.

Lead with compassion

Lead others in a way that lifts them up, rather than beats them down. This requires you to learn how to think in terms of the benefit to your community, not only to yourself.

Lead others to lead themselves

Allow others to develop themselves as leaders through resilience and self-motivation.

━━━━━━━━━━

Lead yourself

The elephant matriarch is a respected leader because she has proven over the years that she can be trusted to make wise decisions and that she is worthy of being their leader.

You don't need a title to be a leader. You are always a leader who is leading yourself through life. To effectively lead others and yourself in a way that garners trust and respect, work on your leadership presence.

As leaders, we like to feel and show that we are in control of a situation, but it's not always easy when we're faced with multiple challenges in our day. In fact, when we are stressed, the pressure often brings out the worst in us, impacting how we manage and lead. Having the type of leadership presence that people can aspire to, takes a conscious effort.

The more aware you are of how you present yourself as a leader, the better you will grow as one. Awareness comes from within. It also comes from others who are watching you, whether you know it or not. It was only when my daughter was starting to say her first words as a toddler that I realized that I said "sh*t" quite a bit. At first, it was alarming and funny to hear that word come out of her mouth. However, it made me more aware that those whom we have the ability to influence pick up on not only our words, but on our attitudes. These attitudes, positive or negative, can have long-lasting effects that can either broaden or limit their perspectives.

Develop your leadership presence

- *Understand what it is*

  Executive Presence is no longer a mystery thanks to Suzanne Bates, CEO of Bates, who championed the first research-based assessment and model of Executive Presence. The *Executive Presence Assessment or ExPI^{TM}* provides a way to measure executive presence using a three-dimensional model of character, substance, and style. It measures perceptions of a leader's strengths and development areas within these dimensions that cover 15 distinct facets, including authenticity, integrity, concern, confidence, composure, and appearance.[3] Even if you aren't an executive, you can still develop these qualities for the benefit of your personal growth, which in turn, will benefit your team and family.

- *Consciously develop it*

  Not all of us are fortunate enough to receive leadership and management training from our employers. I gained most of my management experience from the company I worked for, which provided us with extensive and valuable training. When I was first promoted though, no formal training was immediately included with my new management title. So I made a conscious effort to find role models and to read materials that resonated with my perception of what leadership entailed. One book that stood out—and that I have recommended to many others since—is *The 21 Indispensible Qualities of a Leader: Becoming the Person Others Will Want to Follow* by John C. Maxwell.[4] I loved how he described each quality, and that I could pick a chapter a week and focus on trying to model it to the best of my ability. And they definitely applied to me as a parent too!

There are thousands of leadership and parenting books available, and you can sign up for any number of classes. You've probably read many books and taken seminars on these topics already. I'd encourage you to keep learning and find those that resonate with you.

Look for role models whose behavior you admire and would like to emulate. They can include public figures, other managers in your organization, community members, friends, or relatives. If it is someone you have access to, ask if they are willing to mentor you. Learning directly from someone based on their personal experience can be invaluable. You can have multiple mentors that change over the course of your life. Your relationship with each mentor might differ depending on the nature of the relationship, mentoring topic, and available time.

Most importantly, have fun while you're growing. Don't take yourself too seriously.

Humor and laughter can diffuse many tense situations.

- ***Engage a coach***

  There is a reason professional athletes, especially those at the highest level, have a coach. As skilled as they are, they aren't always able to see their own flaws or which areas need improvement. Even if they can, they need their coach to provide new techniques and to monitor how well they're tweaking or developing a skill. In spite of their success, some of the most successful and respected CEOs of the top 500 companies in the world still have coaches.[5]

  I strongly believe in the value of coaching or I wouldn't have decided to become a certified coach myself. I can clearly see the value of deliberate coaching towards an accomplishment. I now invest in professional coaches for myself because while I have the skills to coach, I want an outside perspective. I want to make the most of each new chapter in my life, and my coaches challenge me in my thinking, while encouraging me to pursue my goal of improving corporate culture.

  In addition, my husband, daughter, son, and close family and friends find opportunities to discuss our current challenges over video calls and when we have a chance to meet in person. We don't always use formal coaching techniques, but we definitely give each other helpful questions and ideas to think about.

━━━━━━━━━━━━━━━━━━

*"Each moment describes who you are, and gives
you the opportunity to decide if that's who you want
to be."*
- iPEC Foundation Principle[6]

━━━━━━━━━━━━━━━━━━

Lead with compassion

A successful elephant matriarch uses her excellent
social skills to maintain strong relationships. She
leads with care and compassion towards the whole
community, making considered decisions for the
safety of the entire herd.

Compassionate leaders see the world from the
other person's perspective. They strive to understand
without being judgmental, recognizing that we've all
walked or climbed a different path. They are
concerned for the well-being of others and aspire to
relieve any suffering, displaying empathy and
humility. Most parents do this naturally, yet they
don't always take this concern to the workplace.

Take a moment to think about all the managers
you've reported to, and about which of them brought
out the best in you. The best leaders are those who
leave you inspired and who you feel "have your
back." They connect with you and encourage you to
grow. They deeply care. While parents deeply care,
not all know how to connect with their children in a
way that inspires.

Neuroscience shows that coaching with compassion towards a positive outcome arouses positive and hopeful feelings in others. The pre-frontal cortex is activated, releasing oxytocin, which is associated with social bonding. Our blood pressure decreases and we feel more hope and joy. In this state, we have enhanced working memory and perceptual openness. Conversely, coaching for compliance induces stress and the release of cortisol. Our blood pressure, heart rate, and breathing rate increase. Emotionally, we feel fear, anxiety, and guilt. Cognitively, we have decreased executive functioning as our brain shuts down non-essential neural circuits. Our openness to change and to learning is reduced. An article published in *Frontiers in Psychology*, describes how a shared vision motivates and inspires people to reach beyond their current state. [7] Doing so requires and produces positive emotions and activation of the parasympathetic nervous system, as opposed to the fight or flight response of the sympathetic nervous system.

Develop mutual trust

Your team and your family want and need to trust you to make decisions that affect their welfare. A study published in *Science Direct* shows that perceptions and intentions of trust affect levels of circulating oxytocin. [8] When the social signal of trust is extinguished, so are the oxytocin response and the degree of trustworthiness. Amongst many other qualities, high-trust leaders are respectful, competent, transparent, loyal, direct, realistic, and accountable.

Trust goes both ways, so those in helicopter and Humvee roles can continue to build that trust each time they have the opportunity to interact. Sometimes, trust has to be rebuilt in order to reestablish a once positive relationship. When you feel your trust has been violated, seek ways to openly discuss the situation, to forgive, and to move forward. This is especially important if the person who has erred shows remorse and corrects their behavior.

Enhance your Emotional Intelligence

Soon after it was first published, our leadership team chose to read *Emotional Intelligence* by Daniel Goleman for our quarterly development assignment.[9] This proved to be extremely helpful when working within our group, and with our project sponsors. Emotional Intelligence (EI or EQ) is the ability to recognize, understand, and manage our own emotions, and the ability to recognize, understand, and influence the emotions of others. Empathy is the ability to understand and share another person's feeling and emotions. It plays a huge role in developing meaningful and productive relationships.

- *Monitor your emotions*

  During the course of the day, monitor when you find yourself despondent or angry; how long the feeling lasts; what triggers it; and what you do to feel better. Assess whether negative emotions you experience or act out on are having an impact on those around you. If you are struggling to overcome them, seek help from a friend or family member, or if necessary, seek professional help. Similarly, monitor when you are feeling happy and energetic. Assess what you are doing at the time and how it reflects in the mood and actions of your team members and family. Emotions are like viruses—they are contagious!

- *Monitor the emotions of others*

  Make a conscious effort to accurately identify and label the emotions of those around you. When unsure, develop skills to ask in a non-threatening and comfortable way rather than make assumptions. Acknowledge any negative emotions they may be experiencing and engage them in respectful conversation to better understand how you may be contributing to how they are feeling. You can't always change the way they feel, but you can change your own behavior if needed.

- *Build positive relationships*

  Instead of an "us *vs.* them" mindset, where possible, adopt an "us *and* them" one. There will always be differences of opinion and we can choose to allow those differences to nurture antagonistic relationships or to cultivate a mindset of collaboration or compromise. We can also choose to walk away from relationships that aren't conducive to becoming more positive over time.

Enhance your Conversational Intelligence®

Leading with Conversational Intelligence® (C-IQ) has a profound and long-lasting impact. In her book *Conversational Intelligence: How Great Leaders Build Trust and Get Extraordinary Results*, author and executive coach, Judith E. Glaser shares that the quality of our conversations can have significant impact in getting to the next level of greatness. Conversations impact relationships and culture. She describes how distinct types of conversations stimulate different parts of our brain to generate feelings of trust or distrust.[10]

- *Change your conversations*

  We have different types of conversations during our interactions with others, depending on what we want to accomplish. However, we may not be aware if we tend to tell people what to do rather than to understand their perspective and jointly agree on a plan of action. Do you use words that demean or uplift others? Do you demand or request? Do you seek to blame or improve? Do you exclude or include others? Do you jump to conclusions or inquire to learn?

  Reflect on the various conversations you have daily at work and at home. Consciously change your conversations towards positively transforming your relationships and your environment by being more collaborative.

Lead others to lead themselves

Imagine if you knew that, no matter what, someone was always there for you; that even if you messed up, that they would "have your back." What an empowering feeling that would be!

Although I wouldn't classify myself as a daredevil, I will say that I have taken many risks in my life. Whether it was emigrating with a young family from Johannesburg to Toronto, Chicago, Irvine, and Jackson Heights (without a pre-arranged job in two of those major moves) or taking on a new and unknown role at work, I always felt that people were looking out for me. Any fears that I had were countered by the feeling of being supported. That, and knowing that I was willing to learn and work hard, helped me to take some bold moves. I'm very fortunate and hope that you are too!

When leading others, allow them to surprise you and themselves by what they are capable of accomplishing on their own.

Develop resilience

In Amy Chua's *Battle Hymn of the Tiger Mother*, we read about an extremely authoritarian and somewhat ruthless parenting style.[11] This attitude was based on the premise that her children were resilient and needed to perform at their absolute best at all times and at all costs, in order to be successful in an increasingly competitive world. She prohibited "frivolous" social activities like sleepovers with friends. However, as extreme as her parenting style was, some basic elements of her approach are supported by psychological and cognitive science research. This research has found that children who have to grapple with difficult tasks have a well-earned sense of mastery and are more optimistic and decisive. That's because they have learned they are capable of overcoming adversity and achieving their goals. However, to develop resilience, they also need at least one person who believes in and supports them during times of stress.[12]

While I don't agree with the harsh treatment Amy Chua sometimes adopted with her children (and some of the outlandish disciplinary methods were exaggerated), I do believe that children are resilient and that we need to find ways to instill discipline and structure tailored to their personal natural styles. For instance, her younger daughter rebelled against the harsh treatment that had worked for the older child, and Ms. Chua eventually backed off ever so slightly. We can also show them that they can overcome problems through diligence, dedication, and analysis, and that they can develop the skills, experience, and motivation to accomplish a goal.

They each have their own personal needs and desires, and we can equip them with life skills to navigate their world at home, at school, at college, in the playground, in the sports field, and eventually in the workplace. They can only cope with what is age-appropriate for them, but they are likely more advanced and capable than we give them credit for.

The work environment can also be tough at times with many challenges to overcome. As long as there is an atmosphere of compassion and respect, managers and employees can understand that there is a business to be run and that there will be times when people will be driven hard to achieve great results.

- *Allow exploration*

  We cannot learn to play tennis by simply watching. We have to pick up a racket and hit the ball over the net ourselves many times before we are ready to play a game. If we only do what we have already mastered, we can't learn and grow. As we are learning, we may find we love it or that we would rather try something else. Exploration allows us to experience different careers, roles, lifestyles, and activities; it also helps us to appreciate the accomplishments of those who have reached a certain level of expertise in something that does not come naturally to us.

- *Allow failure*

  It is important to allow those for whom we feel personally responsible to step out of their comfort zone, even if there is hard work and some risk involved. Failure is not the end consequence. It is a path towards learning responsibility and becoming a better version of you.

  During high school, both of our children had zero period, a class that started at 7 a.m., an hour before the actual school day started. In the first week of a new school term, if they weren't able to get out of bed in time, we woke them up. In the second week, we left them to their own devices and allowed them to be late and incur the penalty - detention. They quickly learned that it was their responsibility to get to school on time every morning - or face the consequences. Our son found he could make it from his bed to the bathroom and downstairs to his car in just over a minute - pretty impressive!

- *Provide a safety net*

  We all need to know that there will be a safety net and that if we fall into it, it will transform into a hammock from where we can contemplate what we learned from the experience. We may decide that we want to try again but with a different approach or we may decide to explore something different.

  At work, when someone takes on a new role for which they aren't quite ready, give them time to battle through and learn from the challenges. Discuss a fallback path so that you don't lose a valued employee simply because the role was a mismatch.

- *Let them work through conflict on their own*

  There are going to be times when disagreement or conflict arises. Where possible allow your children or colleagues to work it out without your intervention. Doing so will help them learn how to see things from another perspective, negotiate, compromise, and collaborate. Assess when you need to interject to facilitate a resolution and/or coach new skills.

Motivate towards self-motivation

One motivation approach more commonly adopted by tiger moms is the "carrot and stick" approach. It offers the combination of a promised reward with a threatened penalty to induce cooperation. Under this authoritarian style, the child is expected to respect the decisions of the mom and to follow the rules without any question. Disobedience is viewed as disrespect and can lead to a power struggle that the child rarely wins. As a result, children don't have the opportunity to discover their own passions and talents.

I personally don't prescribe to the "carrot and stick" approach, because rewards and punishments become associated with an external source and there is no incentive or even ability to rely on self-motivation to achieve a goal.

- *Consider rewards carefully*

  Rewards can come in different forms, but my experience is that they are most effective when aligned with a person's unique motivations and not when they are an end in themselves.

  While some may be effectively motivated by monetary rewards or by being allowed to have more leisure time, this motivation is short-lived and requires a new reward on each occasion. In addition, not all families have the means to dangle a golden carrot. When offered, this type of reward is best coupled with one that has a more long lasting impact.

  Our philosophy is that we send our kids to school/college to get an education, not to get good grades. Good grades are a side benefit of engaging in class and doing their assignments. The real reward is the appreciation of the experience and privilege of a formal education, as well as the personal growth they attain each year. We'd still modestly celebrate their efforts and accomplishments throughout the year, irrespective of their sporting scores or school grades (which still happened to be great!). As adults they are self-motivated, doing what they love and enjoying the journey.

- *Consider consequences carefully*

  Punitive consequences in the form of lost incentives can be disproportionate to the "failure." Even worse, if they are in the form of shame, they can be disheartening and have long-lasting effects. In a recent discussion with our now adult children, they shared they cannot recall ever being punished by us. I think it might be because we typically requested, rather than demanded, a different behavior.

  Both at home and at work if someone is struggling, work with him or her to uncover what concepts weren't understood or what errors were made. Provide the direction or resources to overcome the challenges. Instead of a penalty as a consequence, consider discussing the consequences in terms of a potential missed opportunity or temporary setback to doing what they're passionate about, or in terms of how something they might do could impact others negatively.

- *Don't use guilt*

  Expecting someone to do something out of a sense of guilt is manipulative and self-serving. It places an unnecessary burden on them if they see it as a way to gain your loyalty and love.

- *Ask with appreciation*

  When asking for someone to engage in something, do so with appreciation even though the task has not been accomplished yet. This is especially true if you are asking for someone to go above and beyond their regular duties.

  Although I had participated in many workgroups, this particular one struck me in the way it was set up at the kick off meeting. The leader, and most senior person, had started the session by firmly stating that we were all expected to speak up and offer our ideas. If we failed to do so, he would provide feedback to our managers and it would be reflected in our reviews. While his intention was to motivate us to participate, the punitive incentive resulted in people speaking up simply for the sake of it, trying to outdo each other, and being overly concerned about how their ideas were received.

  A more effective approach would have been to welcome us and thank us for the time we had taken out of our busy schedule to participate. He could have shared that we were selected for the workgroup because we had relevant experience, our opinions were valued, and our complementary skills could improve the current strategy in a meaningful way. I know that I would have been more motivated and excited at the prospect of collaborating towards meeting the objective. I believe the group would have been more focused on doing well together than on looking good.

- ***Encourage the "unnamed" leaders***

  Leaders are all around us, irrespective of their role and title. When a colleague or family member shows the ability to lead a specific area better than you can, allow them to do so and learn from them. Show them how much you value their initiative and their expertise.

"Leadership is a series of behaviors rather than a role for heroes."
- Margaret Wheatley

Key Principle and Action

Become a more compassionate leader

Different situations call for leadership styles that range from autocratic to authoritarian to laissez-faire. However, a management or parenting style that is more democratic and compassionate fosters increased trust and respect. Leaders who also help others to develop resilience and self-motivation in a nurturing way instill a sense of independence and pride.

- Keep developing your leadership presence and leadership skills.
- Lead and coach with compassion and empathy.
- Bring out the leadership qualities in others.

Chapter 3
The Key to the Tree

At age 6, I had a defining moment on a scorching hot summer's day.

"Ching Chong Chinaman!" the curly blond-haired girl chanted, as we played in our local park. "Get off! These swings aren't for you!" she yelled. My older sister and I looked at each other, unsure of what to do. Before we could respond, our next-door neighbor, who had accompanied us to the park, swiftly retorted, "Leave them alone you krulkop! You don't belong here!" Then she grabbed the girl's ice-cream cone and shoved it in her face. Stunned, the

blond girl and her friend ran off. I don't think they expected such a ferocious response, let alone from another white person.

I honestly don't recall anything else about the incident, but the memory resurfaced over 40 years later when it was pointed out to me that I may suffer from an inferiority complex. My feedback provider shared that she believed it was the reason I sometimes rushed through my verbal contributions in a meeting - another defining moment.

As a 3rd-generation Chinese South African who is now a citizen of the United States, I do not take for granted how fortunate I am. My journey to overcome racial taunts and subtle racism pales into insignificance compared to the brutal subjugation that the majority of the population faced under apartheid. Even today, people of all colors still suffer the after-effects of that pernicious, dehumanizing system. The codified system of racial stratification in the apartheid era created a bizarre hierarchy of privilege, which ranked "Whites" at the top, "Blacks" at the bottom and everyone else including "Coloureds" (people of mixed racial heritage) and Asians, including Indians and Chinese, somewhere in between.

Thankfully, with the formation of a new democratic government in 1994, apartheid came to an end. Sadly, a segregationist and separatist mindset remains entrenched in some people, not only in South Africa, but also around the world. Unfortunately, racial, social and class hierarchies persist in all societies.

"For to be free is not merely to cast off one's chains, but to live in a way that respects and enhances the freedom of others."
- Nelson Mandela

The Key to the Tree

Whether we like it or not, family trees and organization charts are hierarchical in nature, ranking one person or group above another according to status, seniority, and authority. Even organizations that adopt a more flat structure have reporting levels. Having a chain of command is usually effective and necessary, but, by its very nature, it can lead to attitudes of entitlement and superiority, and even to unhealthy competition as people scramble over each other to get to the top.

The levels of power, and the importance of these tree structures are, ironically, not mimicked in natural trees. **The quality of the fruit at the bottom is just as good as the fruit at the top**.

Social stratification, family trees, and organization charts are embedded in our lives. We cannot simply chop them down like we can with nature's trees, so we must find ways to collectively thrive in them. **"The Key to the Tree" is *you* and how you choose to behave in it.**

Unlock the Tree

Develop a good understanding of the hierarchical and networked structures in which you exist. Use this knowledge to optimize the structure, better navigate complex ones, and build more purposeful relationships.

Adapt Within the Tree

As new family members are added, or as you and others around you take on new responsibilities, you're constantly shifting your position in a tree. As the tree grows and changes around you, adapt with it.

Enrich the Tree

Irrespective of where you are in a tree, you can enrich it by growing within it. Like a plant, if we aren't growing, we're stagnating or withering away.

Keep the Tree Healthy

No matter where you are in the tree, you play a role in making and keeping it healthy. If you aren't improving the overall quality of the tree are you the dead wood, or the bad apple with a detrimental impact on the rest of the tree?

My first job in my early twenties was with a software company that offered consulting services to large hierarchical organizations. My manager, knowing that I was the most junior and least experienced person on the team, wanted me to feel at ease within the group, and in the presence of customer executives. As we were about to walk into a high-powered meeting, he told me that no matter how important they may seem, I should remember that, "We all look the same sitting on the toilet!" It made me laugh and immediately put me at ease. There are still times when I feel intimidated by, and inferior to others, but it was a huge relief (I couldn't resist) to receive that advice just before the meeting, and so early in my work life.

"I'm not a star! A star is nothing but a ball of gas!"

- Elijah Wood

Unlock the Tree

To function well within a structure, it cannot be a mystery to us. We need to understand it and how others perceive themselves and us in it. Knowing who is part of our structures, and what roles we each have within them, helps to facilitate a shared understanding of responsibilities. We can identify gaps, overlaps, and misalignments in roles. We can also better navigate and build more purposeful relationships in it.

Some structures are very simple and well defined, while others can be extremely complicated and unstable. In large organizations, cross-functional teams, and extended families (such as in-laws, half-siblings, stepfamilies, uncles/aunts, and nephews/nieces), there is a matrixed hierarchy of individuals. These additional branches create a fuller and more abundant, albeit more complex, tree.

The more complex an organizational structure, the more difficult and necessary it is to understand it. We need to know how to navigate within it, otherwise, we can get lost, confused, or forgotten in it, as opposed to actively engaging with a strong network of others who are equally engaged and who can support us.

I have found that building relationships with colleagues outside of my immediate team or industry to be invaluable and enriching. When I became a manager for the first time, the advisors I had who were in different parts of the organization helped me to see some issues more objectively.

When my parents started a small business in Swaziland, my grandmother and live-in housekeeper took care of us in Johannesburg, South Africa, several hours away. Soon after the business opened, my father passed away, leaving my mother to take care of four children between the ages of 4 and 12. I was 11 years old. My mother would drive 4 hours at least twice a month to see us and stock up the freezer. My grandmothers, aunts, uncles, older cousins, and family friends were always on hand to teach us how to cook, take us to school and social events, help us with our homework, and help us get through other aspects of daily living. As a result, even though we are now adults and spread across many continents, I still feel a strong connection to those beyond our immediate family who were there to mentor and guide us. In the same way that my extended family embraced us, we in turn show our nieces and nephews the same bonds of love and support.

Main branch

The main branch, at work and at home, is the core structure in which you mostly operate on a day-to-day basis.

* *Understand and improve the structure*

   Understand the structure in terms of how it is set up to support the objectives of the organization or project. Discuss and make changes that will streamline how people interact and collaborate. Ensure that team members, including you, are positioned in roles aligned with personal development objectives and strengths. While this might take time and cause some disruption at first, in the long run, we can work more effectively when deliberate thought is given to how we're organized.

   You will need to do this periodically given that objectives, projects, and people change. For each project that I managed, I worked with the core participants during the initiation phase to determine how to structure the roles and responsibilities. Together, we could identify gaps that needed to be filled and what skills they personally wanted to enhance through the project. We also clearly communicated the structure to all stakeholders and participants to streamline communication and manage expectations.

If you aren't in a position to make changes, learn who is. You can request a ride in the helicopter or invite them down for a tour in the Humvee. You may not be able to influence a different decision, but you will have a better sense of why they created the structure; you can also give them something to think about.

At home, the family tree defines the structure from the genealogy perspective only. Each group activity has the potential for a new structure. When I did most of the cooking for the family, I was responsible for deciding the menu, shopping, and cooking. Now that my husband has assumed that responsibility, he runs the kitchen and I do the dishes. My son is now a professional chef and when he visits we've learned how to say "Oui chef!"

- *Understand the expectations*
  Each level is associated with a set of responsibilities, and perhaps even with expected deference. Some organizations and families may place greater emphasis on how people at each level should behave and interact within the hierarchy.

  In top down organizations, you may have limited opportunity to influence the structure and you may be expected to follow orders without question. Rank is especially important in the military and you are required to follow a strict chain of command.

In certain cultures, respecting one's elders is of paramount importance in family dynamics. When you are visiting with another family with social norms that are unlike yours, being aware that there may be differences, and respecting those differences, can reduce the risk of offending someone, or of making a social faux pas.

Those at a higher level are expected to make decisions. While you might not always agree with or respect the person, you must respect their role as a decision-maker. As a decision-maker, take your role seriously. Educate yourself on the various aspects that will lead to a more informed and respected decision. Depending on the situation, a decision can be made by the leader - unilaterally and with or without input - or by the team. By recognizing and communicating where on the spectrum a particular decision resides, expectations are set upfront and confusion is avoided.

"You may not always have a choice, but you always have a voice."
- Vicki Lederman

Extended branches

Extended branches are the structures in which you interact on a less frequent basis. Your interaction may be required for mutual support, or it may be initiated for personal enrichment.

- ***Initiate contact***

   Initiate contact with the extended branches directly, or through a mutual association. Social media is definitely a facilitator on the personal front. In fact, it has made me keenly aware of all the members of my extremely large extended family throughout the world, many of whom I have never met. Note to self: Reach out! Professionally, simply invite someone to meet you for coffee or lunch. Communicate why you'd like some time with them, and give them a courteous way to opt out.

- ***Accept the invitation***

   Accepting an invitation to meet someone who has reached out would undoubtedly be appreciated by them, especially if they might have had to build up the courage to do so. You could also be equally enriched by the conversation. If you're unable to meet, you always have the option of an email exchange or of directing them to someone else.

- ***Join in***

   Volunteer for activities at work that are outside of your normal responsibilities. You'd be surprised at how many people you meet later reappear in a completely different collaborative situation years later. In the family context, make the effort to foster connections with extended family when the occasion arises, such as weddings, birthdays and reunions. Cousins are sometimes a child's first friend, and familial bonds strengthen community ties.

- *Get to know each other*
Share information about yourself and ask curious conversations about them. It is so much easier to build upon a relationship when you have an increased understanding of each other that you can nurture over time. In a professional context, come prepared with some questions that you ask in a more conversational than interview style. You may have no other purpose than to simply learn.

- *Be receptive to offers of assistance*
If someone reaches out in good faith to offer assistance, be open and receptive. If you decide to decline their offer, assess whether it's because you have carefully assessed the new information and made a decision based on rational calculations, or if it's simply a result of your pride. By rejecting advice out of hand without considering its merits, you may be missing an opportunity to accelerate your growth or to avoid anticipated pitfalls. The person offering may have more experience in a given area, or is seeing things from a different perspective.

- *Don't meddle*
Even though you might feel like an intimate part of an extended family, you should respect

boundaries. When interacting with the younger generation, remember that acting *in loco parentis* does not actually mean that you replace the parents. There is a thin line between caring for family, and crossing the boundary into meddling. At work, share how you can be of assistance and ask whether your help is wanted. You may not be fully aware of the situation, so be wary of undermining one of your colleagues.

Adapt within the Tree

The Greek philosopher Heraclitus once said that the only constant in life is change. Life changes, we change, others change, relationships change, and structures change. At the same time our positions and roles in each of our structures change. We may initiate some changes, while many result from circumstances that aren't within our control.

Adapting with each generation

In a family tree, even though the generational levels remain the same, the top-down or bottom-up interaction will change. The need to adapt our approach and mindset is particularly important in the context of family dynamics, given the constant and inevitable changes that happen as our grandparents, our parents, our children, and we ourselves grow older.

If we choose not to adapt, we will get stuck in the "in my day..." mindset that prevents us from enjoying what each new generation has to offer. Similarly, learning about the lives of our parents and grandparents when they were younger can help us see them in a different light. For one of her projects, my daughter conducted extensive cross-generation interviews with our family. As a result, she now has a deeper appreciation for how different family members have built resilience and leadership skills while living under apartheid. Each new generation has the profound pleasure of benefitting from the love and lives of those before us. In turn, we do our best to pass our collective wisdom to the next generations and give back to the generations before us. We continue to evolve from hands-on helper to hands-on receiver.

- *Hands-on helper*

  When children are infants, parents have a very *hands-on* approach since there are many things they are unable to do on their own. As they start to respond to verbal and visual cues and develop from toddlers and kindergarteners to lower grade school, we allow them to do more for themselves, accepting that cleaning up spilt milk or re-tying shoelaces is part of the price of teaching independence.

- *Instructor*

  To accelerate their development and establish a basic set of desired behavior, we *instruct* our children, nieces, and nephews. Our tone is still authoritative while including a modicum of choice. Sharing the rationale for the direction provides them with context and the opportunity to think in terms of consequences.

For example: "Please don't touch the settings on the alarm because it might not ring when we need it to, and we'll be late for the game." As opposed to "GET AWAY FROM THAT!"

- *Guide*

   Along the way, we are also *guiding* the younger generation and helping to establish their core values. We teach them to tell the truth, what it means to be fair and respectful, to have basic manners, how to refrain from harming themselves and others, how to use their words and not their fists to communicate, and all other aspects of what are considered to be acceptable social norms and mores. They, in turn, accept that you will stand by them, that your responses to their actions are reasonable, that you give them opportunities to try things that are new and different. They also learn that they too have responsibilities at home, and that responsibilities are one of the precepts of family life – everyone, even the youngest member, has a part to play in the running of a harmonious household. Above all, to err is part of being human and that mistakes are a part of learning.

- *Mentor*

   As children grow up, they naturally test limits and become more independent. At times, they may be willfully disobedient and stubborn;

particularly, as any parent can attest, in their teenage years. While to some degree, we still need to direct and guide them, at this stage of their lives, if we have instilled good values, they should know, at least on an intellectual level, what they ought to do or not do. (Their emotions, however, will continue to be a challenge). As they mature, they will want, and perhaps need, to do it their way. As we recognize this happening, we have the opportunity to modify our dialogue and tone. We want to be considered not only as an instructor, but also a *mentor* who can dispense advice based on our accumulated wisdom and experience. We want them to know that we trust them to explore and make decisions on their own. Will they make mistakes? Definitely. Will they learn from their mistakes? Hopefully. Will they call for help? Maybe. Will you be there if they need you? Absolutely.

- *Peer*

Our mentoring role really never ends and we'll always be their parents. However, as they become young adults we shift to having conversations with our children as *peers*. It may be hard for us to accept that we can't really make them do things. They have their own lives to lead and decisions to make. Like a trusted advisor, we can only help them see the pitfalls and possibilities. The final choices they make are all their own.

- *Mentee*

  While it might be difficult to let go of our children, consider the upside. The world they are independently exploring is completely different to the one we explored at their age. They are having experiences that weren't available to us. This is the time for us to be *mentees* and embrace them as our mentors who can open up a vista of possibilities and wonderment in our lives.

  My daughter attended NYU, creating her own major in The Politics of Language at the Gallatin School of Individualized Study. She epitomizes what it means to be part of the "slash generation." As a UX designer and story strategist/writer and a former reporter/copywriter, she shows me how to navigate having multiple parallel careers that play to my different strengths and interests. My son graduated with a degree in behavioral neuroscience at Northeastern University. He is now following his passion as a chef at Boston's premier fine dining restaurant. He keeps us up to date with the culinary arts as well as popular culture. The point is that they both forged their own paths and showed us that second acts are not only possible; they can lead to growth and personal fulfillment.

- *Hands-on receiver*

  As we age, we may find that we are no longer able to do certain things for ourselves. Old age sneaks up on us. We might feel too proud to ask for help. We may see it as an imposition to ask for assistance in driving us around or performing what were once routine chores. This is the time to learn to accept our limitations and to ask for help.

Adapting professionally

In our professional lives our relative positions to others is ever-changing as we move into different roles or levels. As a result, we will also find ourselves changing from hands-on helper to hands-on receiver multiple times.

As I reflect upon my own personal and professional growth, I feel extremely fortunate that I was nurtured along similar paths at home and at work. Assistance was always available as I changed positions in the corporate structure, even if it was to help me become more resourceful on my own. This is the reason I try to do the same for others, whether it is part of my official responsibility to help them or not. And like those who have helped me, I do not give of my time or knowledge with the expectation of a quid pro quo.

Evolving from hands-on helper to hands-on receiver is how I approach my role as a manager at work. When I first became a manager, I was uncomfortable, initially, being the "boss." I quickly realized that I could still effectively manage a team, department, or project by recognizing when I needed to be hands-on giver, instructor, guide, mentor, peer, mentee, or hands-on receiver. I was lucky to work with a group of colleagues who were each smarter or more skilled than I was in at least one area, and who were willing to share their time and knowledge with me. There are times when I didn't get it quite right. Each time I moved into a new role to lead a different team, I had to learn another line of business, technology, and set of processes. When my skills were not yet up to par, I asked and relied on my colleagues to be patient with me. I also appreciated when they stepped in to guide me. They did not think any less of me as a leader for admitting my limitations and asking for help.

With each new role at work, ask yourself if you are doing the same things you were doing in your prior role. If so, should you be delegating some of them to someone on your team so that they can grow, and should you be challenging yourself to do different types of work in your new role? If you are still responsible for doing some of the same work, is there a different way in which you could be approaching it and are you reaching out to others for recommendations?

Now that I am a certified professional coach, I am learning how to adapt to a whole new tree structure in the coaching and entrepreneurial world. I'm excited to have the opportunity to enrich the tree as I grow in it.

"Leadership is an action, not a position."
- Donald McGannon

Enrich the Tree

While we naturally strengthen the tree when we adapt within it, we can further enrich it by growing within it, and by helping others to do the same.

Growing where you are

Whether because of lack of desire or opportunity to grow to the next level, we can still keep growing from where we are. If we don't grow, we stagnate, and from there, we deteriorate.

- *Grow your skills and contribution*

    Keep growing your skills and knowledge so that you can elevate your performance and contribute in more impactful ways. Advances in technology and thinking will continue to redefine how we accomplish an objective so your skills may need to be upgraded. While job security is never guaranteed, strong performance plays a big factor. Ongoing education is a win-win for you and the organization. Similarly at home, learn how to use new technologies not only to make your personal life more efficient, but also to give you access to an abundance of online resources. Your family can be enriched together.

- *Share with others*

    Children have contradictory impulses. At first their world is small and everything revolves around them and their own needs. They also demonstrate altruism that becomes apparent as they start to interact with others. At this stage,

we encourage them to share their toys and learn
to play nicely with others, further developing
their sense of community and social
responsibility. In fact, research done by the
Proceedings of the National Academy of
Sciences of the United States of America shows
that very simple reciprocal activity elicited high
degrees of altruism in children ages 1–2 years
and older, and that friendly but nonreciprocal
activity did not.[13]

As they grow older, they are placed in
competitive situations, some healthier than
others. We try to teach them about compromise
and good sportsmanship, yet this mindset doesn't
always transfer into other life situations. The
survival instinct sometimes trumps magnanimity.

Unfortunately, the competitive culture of
some organizations is a disincentive to share
your knowledge and experience with others.
However, to build a good network of trusted
relationships and to work in the spirit of
collaboration, share what you can with others to
enrich the work environment.

Growing to the next level

We all have personal motivations for growing to the
next level at work, yet some of us do so in a manner
that destroys, instead of nourishes, the tree. Once at a
higher level, some use their position to create positive
change while others use it as a way to further their
personal agenda.

In family trees, new generations automatically
move us up the tree. With each new family addition,

we grow into our roles and can enrich our families with skills we grow along the way. Age bestows seniority, but not necessarily wisdom; so make sure you are worthy of deference by upholding values that engender respect.

As you grow to the next level, ask yourself whether you are enriching or poisoning the tree.

- *Consider your motivation*

  There are many reasons for wanting to get to the next level, including progressing along your career path, having a broader sphere of influence, or having a sense of accomplishment. However, if you are driven by one-upmanship, peer pressure, or the need to prove yourself to others, ask yourself why that step up matters so much to you and whether it is aligned with what you truly value. While the promotion would be beneficial to the organization and to you in the short term, you might not be as fulfilled in the long term. Unless you can find personal meaning in a new role, you will not be as actively engaged to enrich the tree.

- *Reflect on the cost to others*

  If you are knowingly climbing up the corporate ladder at the expense of others, reflect on how you would feel if you were the rung and not the foot. Others don't have to lose for you to win. Attempting to justify self-serving actions will garner alienation instead of loyalty. You may get away with mistreating others for a time, but your machinations will soon become obvious to those around you and you will find yourself without allies when you need them.

- **_Bring others along_**

  As you reach positions of higher responsibility and influence, bring others along with you. Instead of competing, seek ways to support and lift others. Leverage your new connections to share job openings. The saying: "a rising tide lifts all boats" does not only apply to macro economic policy. Create opportunities for your colleagues to grow along with you. Help them to create a vision for their own career. They may even be promoted above you, but by creating a culture of mutual support, you can reduce toxicity in the workplace. You can choose to jealously protect your tiny fiefdom, or to allow your whole team to share in even greater success.

- **_Stay connected_**

  Don't forget that most of the people you worked with and who reported to you have in some way contributed to your personal success. Stay genuinely connected with them, as they will often be the ones who will give you the best and most honest insight, advice, and feedback. You can also connect them to new opportunities across the organization.

  As your children and parents keep growing into new versions of themselves, stay connected. If not, you run the risk of becoming strangers, or not knowing when they might need your support.

You can also better appreciate each other's personal journeys, and guide each other as needed.

- ***Don't feel pressure to be "perfect"***

    When people are looking up to you, it is hard not to feel the pressure of being perfect. You have reached a level of accomplishment with all your flaws and by being perfectly imperfect. We are all fallible and are expected to make mistakes as we grow. Strive to be the best version of yourself and the person you want to be. Owning up to mistakes and imperfections, and showing vulnerability is not a weakness. It gives your team license to admit to their own mistakes - and that could be the difference between the success and failure of a project or mission. Imperfectly shaped apples are as tasty as those shined with wax.

Keep the Tree Healthy

As our position in a hierarchical structure changes, so may our perceived level of importance. Some people who have accomplished extraordinary achievements in their lives can become more egotistical, while others remain humble.

I think of Richard Branson[14], founder of the Virgin group, business magnate, philanthropist, and adventurer, who has accomplished so much, yet leads with discretion and humility, rather than with arrogance and ego. He is such a sharp contrast to the stereotype of an obnoxious parent at the soccer game or the corporate shark in the boardroom. Humble leaders are respected because they are considerate of others and do not allow their egos to belittle others.

Entrepreneur Naveen Jain shared a story of when Richard Branson invited him to visit Necker Island, which included an invitation to enjoy the watersports. When Richard Branson learned that Naveen Jain could not swim, the Virgin magnate spent hours patiently teaching him the skills to do so. Naveen Jain writes, *"And it was Sir Richard Branson himself, the man behind numerous multinational companies bearing his Virgin brand around the world, a vast personal network, an immeasurable empire and indeed, one of the busiest men on the planet, who took many hours out of this week to teach me how (I am 53 years old). Those moments don't come often as we get older. I will be forever grateful to Branson for showing me the utmost humility as I took those first laps in wonder."*[15]

No matter where we are in a structure, we need to be careful not to blindly defer, or automatically listen to, the person with the loudest voice or the highest rank. We owe it to ourselves to seek out instead, those with real insight and substance.

- **Stay rooted**

  As proud as you are of your accomplishments, keep your sense of self-importance in check. If you have made a valuable contribution, trust that it will be recognized. If it is not, others may not be aware of what you have achieved. You may even want to seek an environment that recognizes the contributions of all. Resist the urge to be seen as the know-it-all or to downplay the contributions of others. Don't invite ego to the celebration and don't expect others to feed your ego.

As you develop and move up the corporate ladder, don't think that others are literally beneath you. While you may be in a more responsible and better-compensated position, you are simply playing your role in the company, along with everyone above and below you in the hierarchy. Remember that the smallest cog still plays an essential role in the running of a machine. Solicit and value input and ideas from everyone in the organization, irrespective of their title or position.

When you become a parent, resist placing expectations on your children to treat you as king or queen of the castle with ultimate power. Family members should not be expected to do things for you based on a sense of your personal entitlement. See yourself as part of the team and pitch in along with everyone else towards the day-to-day running of the household. Within a family, everyone has a role to play, according to their capabilities.

At home, this should be no different. Parents and children can show mutual appreciation of everyone's suggestions. Although parents ultimately have the power to decide, children's suggestions should be accorded more than lip service. By not being ignored or left out of the decision making process, children have more of a stake in outcomes, which is essential to a healthy family dynamic. In more traditional spousal relationships, the expectation of submission disempowers great minds.

- *Don't demand respect*

   If you feel you are not being accorded the respect you deserve and feel the need to demand it because of your place in a hierarchical structure, contemplate whether you are behaving in a way that is hampering your ability to earn it. Your actions will demonstrate that you are worthy of leadership, not the petty accoutrements of higher office. Your team will look up to you because you demonstrate fortitude and coolness under pressure, not because you have a coffee mug proclaiming you to be the world's greatest boss. Remember that people who place less importance on hierarchies will not feel the need to treat you in a special way.

   Whether you are in your work or family structure, maintain the same positive tone. Ask yourself if you are harsher with your immediate family than you are with your team and vice versa. Your loved ones deserve the same level of respect and interaction as your colleagues.

- *Speak up*

   The person who is nominally the most senior in the room does not always have the best ideas or the most knowledge. There are ways to raise objections, or question decisions respectfully, without being insubordinate. When you don't agree with those in higher positions, you owe it to yourself and others to speak up calmly and rationally.

Unfortunately, in some organizations or groups, this may be seen as a career-limiting move that makes us more reluctant to do so. By not speaking up, we become actively disengaged and gripe to our colleagues, to our trusted friends, or more damagingly for the employer, on company review websites. If we are leading others, who are looking to us to speak up and we fail to look out for their interests, we may rightfully be perceived as cowardly, and lose their respect. Of course, those in helicopter roles are responsible for setting a tone that encourages open and honest dialogue.

"We all should know that diversity makes for a rich tapestry, and we must understand that all the threads of the tapestry are equal in value no matter what their color."

- Maya Angelou

Key Principle and Action

Be a positive impact in hierarchical structures

While hierarchical structures exist in society, you do not need to have a hierarchical mindset that leads to feelings of entitlement, superiority, or inferiority. The key is to acknowledge the tiers and find ways to navigate your way through them. How you see yourself and how you treat others is a far greater distinguisher of character and personal progress, than your rank in a hierarchy.

- Understand the structures in which you exist and optimize them for the benefit of all.

- Continually adapt to changes in hierarchical structures as they change and grow around you.

- Grow in all the structures that you're in and bring others along with you.

- Ensure that your role, attitude, and relationships within structures impact them in a positive manner.

Chapter 4
One Size Fits All... Except When It Doesn't

Many years ago I attended a pro basketball game, when the L.A. Lakers still played at the Great Western Forum. By that time, the stadium was on its last legs, creaky and decrepit, but the acoustics were great, magnifying every chant of "DE-FENSE!" to a roar and reaching a crescendo when Magic Johnson made a patented no-look over the shoulder pass on a fast break.

Unfortunately, the seats were hard and uncomfortable, and perched in the thin air of the nosebleed seats, my legs felt cramped and restricted.

At just a little over 5' tall, I could hardly be described as long legged, so I commiserated with the man on my left who looked to be at least 6'3", folded like a contortionist in the same plastic seat.

A few years later I caught another game at the $375 million Staples Center, the brand new home of the Lakers. The arena was modern and luxurious as befitted the (then) 14-time NBA Championship team. The carpeting was plush, the private boxes were gleaming altars to the sponsors, and the concession prices were exorbitant. Unfortunately, when I got to my seat in the second tier, I found that the hard materials and small dimensions of the seats had not been upgraded. A few pre-teen fans could happily swing their legs; everyone else was twisted like a pretzel. It was obvious that the person planning the seating was focused on maximizing capacity rather than ergonomic comfort. Whenever the Lakers scored, everyone stood up - not only to cheer, but also as an excuse to stretch their legs.

I was reminded of the story of Procrustes. In Greek mythology, he kept a house by the side of the road where he offered hospitality to passing strangers. He invited travelers in for a pleasant meal and a night's rest in his very special bed. Procrustes described it as having the unique property that its length exactly matched whomsoever lay down upon it. What the host neglected to tell them was the method by which this "one-size-fits-all" was achieved—namely that as soon as the guest lay down, Procrustes went to work upon him, stretching him on the rack if he was too short for the bed and chopping off his legs if he was too long. Nobody was ever the right size for the bed.

―――――――

One Size Fits All... Except When It Doesn't

You could have heard a pin drop. Each person in the wood-paneled auditorium was listening intently to the then 90-year-old legendary Coach John Wooden[16] as he flawlessly recited from one of his favorite poems *They ask me why I teach*, by Glennice L. Harmon, which ends with this line: "They ask me why I teach, and I reply,/ 'Where could I find more splendid company?'"[17]

When I was working for a splendid company, I was fortunate enough to hear the retired coach speak to the representatives and clients of the Los Angeles-based group. Although I knew little about Wooden before that day, it was clear to see why he was one of the most revered coaches in the history of sports and why so many were inspired by his coaching philosophy.

As a basketball coach, Wooden was a stickler for rules including: never be late, be neat and clean, no profanity, never criticize a teammate, never make excuses, and never grandstand, loaf, sulk, or boast. When a young Bill Walton expressed that, as player of the year, he should be allowed to grow his hair longer than Wooden's 2-inches rule, the coach responded that while he didn't have the right to tell

Bill to cut his hair, he had the right to choose who was going to be on the team, and that he would miss Bill. Immediately Bill jumped on his bike and raced off to the barbershop hoping to make it back to practice before the coach realized he was late. When it came to his rules, Wooden was unwavering in the philosophy of "One Size Fits All."

Certainly every sports coach has rules and a set of standards that they expect everyone to adhere to. However, the leadership styles of both Phil Jackson and Gregg Popovich are great examples of how "One Size Fits All... Except When It Doesn't" taps into the uniquely special strengths of each individual athlete.

When Phil Jackson coached the Chicago Bulls and the Los Angeles Lakers, he carefully selected books he thought would best motivate and connect with each member of the team. He gave Michael Jordan a Toni Morrison novel, Shaquille O'Neal a book by German philosopher Nietzsche, and Kobe Bryant *Blink* by Malcolm Gladwell. He never explained why he paired a particular book with a player, so his selections were probably puzzling to the players. His reputation as a Zen Master coach surely had them consider his motivations. Ultimately, he wanted to help his players discover their own talents and create a role for themselves on the team aligned with those talents. Now that he is president of the New York Knicks, he still hands out a thoughtfully compiled team summer reading list.

Gregg Popovich, coach of the San Antonio Spurs since 1996, has the reputation of being one of the greatest coaches in the history of the NBA. Like Wooden, his focus is on building character in a player and not merely on winning games. Popovich is known for how well he creates his system to complement the unique talents of the team at the time. His philosophy is to maximize the value of the talent he has on his team, adapting his strategy as needed to tap into those talents. He also emphasizes and expects flexibility from his team to handle different situations on the court. Unlike Procrustes, he does not subscribe to a system that enforces uniformity or conformity without regard to individuality.

For me, the term "One size fits all" conjures up the cartoon image of an elephant and a mouse both wearing the same hat. It teeters on the elephant's head and engulfs the mouse's entire body. Fortunately, hats for humans come in various sizes, but assuming we can each find a hat that fits us perfectly, we'd only feel comfortable wearing ones that match our personality or the task at hand.

When "One Size Fits All" applies

The law and rules apply equally and consistently to everyone. If there is some leeway, then they can be seen as guidelines to be applied fairly based on the situation.

When "Except When It Doesn't" applies

While each of us can adopt a leadership style that works for our personality and situation, we also need to appreciate that what works when interacting with one person might not work with another.

To the extent that we can recognize when and how to tailor our core authentic approach, we can build deeper relationships that respect the unique attributes of each person. **By tailoring our interactions, requests, and expectations, we allow each person to feel really good about their core innate abilities and strengths, allowing them to blossom based on their unique characteristics and on what brings meaning to their lives**.

"Success is peace of mind which is a direct result of self-satisfaction in knowing you made the effort to become the best you are capable of becoming."
-   John Wooden

When "One Size Fits All" applies

When it comes to rules, a **"One Size Fits All"** model applies. Rules define what is allowed and not allowed in a particular situation. They are non-negotiable and have consequences if not followed. There are occasions where absolute compliance is not required, yet certain actions or behaviors are more desirable than others. In these situations, you set guidelines. They're less rigid and provide recommendations. Ideally they should be consistently followed and any deviations should be discussed to understand the broader consequences. You should also communicate the rationale for conditional inconsistency to avoid confusion.

Establish rules and guidelines

Rules and guidelines need to be established in advance. Your role as a leader is not a license to demonstrate your power or control over others. It is to assess where rules matter and requires that you make informed and rational decisions. Rules and guidelines exist to serve and facilitate the completion of tasks according to desired standards, rather than to hinder them.

- *Right size them*

  If you have too many rules, or rules that are too restrictive, you will spend most of your time in a battle of the wits with the rule-breakers instead of making progress. No one wants to be constantly told what to do, especially when the rules don't seem reasonable to them. People are more likely to respect rules if they perceive that your approach stems from a consistent application of rules that are fair-minded and not arbitrary.

  Depending on the organization and the family, an element of desired behavior may be placed in the rules or the guidelines category.

  When possible, allow flexibility, recognizing that needs, circumstances, and people constantly change, sometimes beyond our control. For example, if you allow flexible working hours or work from home, allow each person to assess what would work best for them personally while also meeting business needs. If you want your children to learn to play a musical instrument, let it be one aligned to their preferences while recognizing that unlimited choice is not always possible or desirable amongst young children who perhaps require some guidance.

• *Communicate them*
Some norms will require explicit communication and others may evolve organically. Either way, rules should not be enforced in an authoritarian manner and with an attached ultimatum.

I thought my husband came up with a smart idea when our children were little. He told them with excitement and a smile, "You kids are really lucky. Most families have lots of rules about all kinds of things, but in our family we only have one rule and it's a simple one. All we ask is that you listen to mom and dad." To their young minds, this sounded awesome! Before 7:30 p.m. every evening, we would gently remind them that bedtime was coming up soon and they should start to wrap up what they were doing and pack their toys away. Without any battles, they made their way upstairs within 10 minutes for bath time and story time, which we also made fun. We still met the overall objective without the notion of demanding that they be in bed by 8 p.m. or else…! On weekends or evenings when we had guests or events, we didn't feel bound by a set of rules that we ourselves could not adhere to. Through this they learned flexibility and the ability to get back on track afterwards.

- ***Evolve them***

  Rules and guidelines that are applicable today may not be applicable in the future. Even though there were numerous management meetings about what constituted appropriate business casual attire, I was extremely happy when we moved away from suits, ties, and pantyhose. In the spirit of common sense and progress, periodically assess the rules to determine what no longer applies, what needs to be tweaked, and where new ones are needed. To avoid confusion there should be some communication that they've been changed. If you make changes, be consistent in how you apply them or you'll come across as indecisive and ineffectual.

When "Except When It Doesn't" applies

"**Except When It Doesn't**" applies when, by treating everyone in the same way, regardless of circumstance, we are not being fair to them. As with Phil Jackson and Gregg Popovich, we can tailor our interaction and expectations of others to bring out their natural strengths, while helping them to overcome their weaknesses.

To be fair requires us to learn more about the other person so that we can be reasonable, open-minded, and unbiased, while taking into account their different backgrounds, personalities, characteristics, strengths, interests, and aptitudes.

Understanding your "Fair Factor"

Before you can tailor your approach, acquire a better understanding of the person you are interacting with and of any biases (conscious or unconscious) you may have that may be hampering or enhancing your ability to be fair.

- *Recognize your biases*

  Whether we like it or not, we all have biases that inform our initial assumptions. Unconscious biases lead us to fill in the blanks for ourselves and create limitations in our thinking. When people don't look like us, we immediately make an assessment that labels them. Where possible, have a discussion with others about any decision you are making to ensure that it does not arise from an unconscious bias that negatively impacts others or perpetuates a stereotype. I'm embarrassed to admit that in a recent conversation, I incorrectly assumed that the CIO we were discussing was male. In that moment I realized that I simply associated that role with a male. I wonder how my other unconscious biases are showing up without the ability to monitor them, and what impact they have on my actions.

- *Resist the temptation to judge*

  We tend to judge others based on our own value system, beliefs, and past experiences. We categorize their words or actions as good/bad or right/wrong. Given the right combination of circumstances, we could escalate a simple disagreement with a colleague or family member into a full blown argument or come away from the encounter nursing resentments. Those resentments may metastasize into a grudge that taints all our future interactions with them and unnecessarily consumes our emotional energy.

To be fair to both parties, discuss your differences calmly and rationally. If you don't know, ask questions to better understand which of their core values were in conflict with yours. Accept that they are entitled to their own belief system and be open to changing yours. Be respectful of their choices, even if you cannot reconcile them with yours.

On one of his weekend visits, my son and I had the opportunity to experience a conflict in our values. He was teaching me how to make ravioli like he made it in the fine dining restaurant where he worked. As he was cutting the shapes, I started to gather the irregular strips of discarded pasta into a pile so I could boil them up and make another small meal out of them. He looked at me quizzically and asked why I was keeping the scraps. When I told him, he got slightly agitated that I was holding onto a few cents worth of flour and eggs that were only fit for the trashcan. After a bit of back-and-forth dialogue, he shook his head and threw the scraps away. We had a little laugh at our minor tiff and continued with the task at hand.

Later that day, I shared with him that what transpired was a result of our different values around food. I grew up in a household were my grandmother who lived with us was constantly reminding us to switch off the lights when we left a room. If we forgot, she would come behind us and switch them off herself. We generally lived a frugal lifestyle and we never threw food away. On the other hand, while we also raised our children to not waste, my son now has a different mindset regarding food. Originality and superior quality are an expectation in his kitchen at work. Even the slightest imperfection is not acceptable. Because I understood that what he valued was different to what I did, and that neither of us was "right" or "wrong," I chose to let it (in this case, the pasta) go. I also encouraged him to approach the next conflict situation that arises with a greater awareness of how he might be judging others in terms of his own values.

Being Fair

"It's not fair!" is an outburst we've all heard, if not said or thought ourselves. Often, this is followed by: "Well, life's not fair!", a statement that is all too true. While many situations are out of our control, being fair in how we personally treat others is something we can all do.

- ***Even the odds***

  Sometimes, unfair treatment may work in our favor. We need to recognize when that occurs and that even though we benefit, someone else may be adversely impacted. Assessing whether we knowingly or unknowingly gain personal benefit at the expense of others affords us the opportunity to even out the situation when appropriate and when it is in our power to do so. A practical example is determining a player's handicap in amateur golf to allow players of different skills to play against each other on somewhat equal terms.

- *Pay fairly*

  When you have assessed that two people with similar backgrounds and expertise are consistently performing at a similar level, but that their compensation is noticeably different, don't try to get away with paying less. Pay others fairly and hope that those who have a say in your compensation are doing the same for you.

- *Don't play favorites*

  Whether it is to alleviate guilt, to offset a disadvantage, or for any other reason, we may find ourselves overcompensating to the extent that it appears we are playing favorites. Coach Wooden believed that everyone on his team had the capacity to compete, realize their full potential, and contribute to the greater good of the team. He applied this philosophy to his starting five and benchwarmers alike.

- *Beware of comparisons*

  It's difficult not to compare when assessing how to be fair-minded with two very different people. In fact, it may even be necessary to understand how we need to adjust our interactions with each. However, beware of comparisons that move towards judgments rather than considerations for leveling the playing field. Parents may blurt out, "Why can't you be more like…" without considering the long-term damage such a cruel statement may have on their child's sense of self worth.

- *Beware of labels*

  While it can be helpful to categorize behaviors—perhaps in order to identify or discuss them—be cautious of labeling or pigeonholing an individual. Labels by their very nature are restrictive, not only for the person labeled, but for the person doing the labeling. Labeling has a tendency to close the mind to other possibilities. People constantly change and grow, and you need to periodically monitor if your perception of them is outdated.

- *Walk in their shoes*

  You can't expect everyone to react the same way in every situation. Cultural, family, and personal background and circumstances are unique to each individual. To "walk in someone else's shoes" is to truly empathize with them, and until you can do that, you will never know what factors influence their actions. Make an effort to get to know people better, if you are going to interact with them on a continuing basis, and not just in the context of your current relationship with them.

At work, even though there are basic expectations of each job function, not every manager, analyst, doctor, chef, or customer service representative is going to bring the same skills to the role.

There are some people in technical roles that have amazing technical skills. They are the ones who crack the toughest problems and devise impactful and elegant solutions. However, if they do not also have dynamic presentation skills or if they avoid the limelight, those who value the ability to be a vibrant presenter can diminish their accomplishments. On the other hand, a manager who is assessing them on narrow criteria may give a disproportionately higher performance review to a mediocre technologist with the gift of the gab.

To be fair, we need to better understand and appreciate that each individual brings something unique to the table, and we should encourage and reward their natural talents and the overall impact they make. This will not only make them feel valued, but it will also help them along a path that is better aligned with their strengths and preferences. We need to build complementary teams that can deal with every possibility, while simultaneously encouraging different perspectives and mutual appreciation.

At home, no two families, grandparents, parents, and children are alike. We can help our children understand that what works for one family may not work for another, especially when they start to recognize that their classmates have different family structures, schedules, and ground rules. By providing them with a broader view of life beyond their family bubble early in life, we can help them see that "One

Size Fits All… Except When It Doesn't" allows them
to be themselves, only better!

────────────────

Key Principle and Action

Embrace and develop natural strengths

Enforced rules are critical when consistency and a
level of standards are required. Guidelines provide
more situational flexibility and should be applied in
the spirit of fairness. However, when it comes to
motivating others to reach their full potential, you
can't force a square peg into a round hole. Taking the
time and effort not only to understand the unique
strengths, weaknesses, and desires of each individual,
but also to help them nurture their positive attributes
and passions, can have a greater impact on their
personal growth and happiness.

- Re-visit your rules and guidelines, and
  communicate any changes you make as you
  right size them.

- Treat others fairly by being reasonable, open-
  minded, unbiased, and non-judgmental.

- Tailor your interactions and expectations to
  further develop the innate strengths of your
  family and team members.

Chapter 5
Latitude in Your Attitude

I sigh to myself as I watch them silently steaming at each other. What began as a minor annoyance will probably ruin their commute, if not their day.

The first woman looks annoyed at having to make her way through the morning crowd. She finds a spot just in front of me and places her larger bag beside her feet before holding onto the rail. The second woman is seated with her legs crossed and slightly angled into the center aisle. Engrossed in her phone, she is oblivious to the morning shuffle and the bag placed just a few inches away from her foot. It's a pretty standard NYC scene - a train full of strangers up close and personal, trying to mind their own business. Except when they can't.

As the train leaves the station, the standing woman looks down. "Could you please sit properly?" she says in a soft yet demanding tone. The seated woman peers up from her phone and then down to her legs, and replies, "I am." She makes no attempt to move her feet, but her attempt to ignore the request is futile. They are both clearly miffed by the exchange, mired in their own indignant righteousness.

I resist the urge to go into "mommy mode" myself. I imagine the teachable moment I might have seized upon had they been my own young children. I ponder if these are some lessons I would share: in crowds, you can expect to be squashed and bumped, so unless someone is going out of their way to make it more unpleasant, deal with it; remember that there are times when you might unintentionally or unknowingly bother someone - when they point it out, simply apologize; if you need to ask someone to move, be friendly and polite, but understand that they might not be able to or want to; if someone asks you to accommodate them and it's simple enough, just do it; if they're rude, you don't have to be; unless someone is in harm's way, mind your own business; and when the train door slams shut just as you were about to enter, simply stand back and wait for the next one. I also think about the stop-and-go commute I used to have on the 405-freeway in Los Angeles and imagine every 100th car flaming with road rage.

And then, the idea of the power of encouraging a "Reachable Moment" pops into my head. If a teachable moment is defined as the time at which learning a particular topic or idea becomes possible or easiest, a "Reachable Moment" is the time at which we choose to go high, not low. It is the time at which attaining a higher state of mind becomes a natural tendency. It is the moment in which we don't become angry or anxious about a situation. We handle it calmly, rationally, and without judgment or offense.

Latitude in Your Attitude

An attitude is a settled way of thinking or feeling about someone or something that defines how we behave. While we can settle on an immediate plan of action or a decision, having an embedded way of thinking prevents us from opening our minds to new and different possibilities. We judge others, and ourselves, gently or harshly. Our ideas become ossified and we find ourselves unable to retreat from a position even when compelling new information comes to light.

Having some **"Latitude in Your Attitude"** can help free us from limiting notions or inclinations that prohibit productive conversations with others, and hold us back in our personal and professional growth. There are a few areas where making a small mental shift can make a significant impact to your life.

"Good" and "bad" are boxes we've created that inhibit our ability to shift.

Bad skills happen to good people

Recognize that those with bad skills don't set out to be incompetent. Their ineptness does not necessarily reflect on their character. Similarly, when you are not at your best, you probably won't want people to use those times to form an overall impression about you.

Good behavior does not negate bad behavior

Bad behavior cannot simply be undone by a single instance of good behavior if the bad behavior continues. It must be corrected or stopped.

An Attitude of Gratitude

Expressing gratitude is a powerful way to elevate our mood and our well-being. Putting life into perspective is a key ingredient to our happiness.

"Your attitude, not your aptitude, will determine your altitude."

- Zig Ziglar

Bad skills happen to good people

Unfortunately, there will always be those in positions of power who are incorrigibly self-serving and distrustful, undeserving of respect as they manipulate and take advantage of others. Think about the corruption that is so prevalent in many organizations and governing bodies around the world that it has become a regrettably accepted part of life.

Fortunately, most people who behave badly are not necessarily evil. Bad skills can and do happen to good people. In these circumstances, we can show some latitude in how we work with others when they are not at their best. We can give others the benefit of the doubt knowing that no one deliberately sets out to do a bad job. We can also give ourselves some leeway when we are not at our best.

When *others* aren't at their best

If we find ourselves developing a negative attitude towards an authority figure whom we don't view as a "good" manager or parent, consider giving them some leeway. Try to understand why they do the things that they do, or make the decisions they make and perhaps your attitude and relationship towards them will become more positive. Remember, no one is perfect.

- *Assess intent*

  In many cases, people will make mistakes due to lack of experience or to an oversight. Before concluding that someone's actions arise from malicious intent or from a self-serving agenda,

assess whether you are making assumptions
about their motives. Ask questions to better
understand their position, and also to clarify if
you are making the right presumptions. Also,
remember that when people are under stress,
they may act out without considering the effect
they have on others.

- *Reflect on yourself*

   When you see flaws in others, do some earnest
   reflection on whether you are inclined to have
   similar shortcomings. Sometimes, the reason the
   bad behavior in others resonates with us, is
   because we may subconsciously recognize
   elements of that behavior in ourselves. I
   sometimes silently criticize others for allowing
   their work to consume their lives—until I realize
   that I am occasionally guilty of the same thing.

- *Be sensitive*

   Be sensitive to their feelings and resist the urge
   to ridicule. Making fun of someone publicly or
   privately, especially when they're not at their
   best or not acting according to your personal
   standards, will ultimately reflect more negatively
   on you. The idioms "Two wrongs don't make a
   right," and "An eye for an eye makes the whole
   world blind" may be clichés, yet they are rooted
   in the basic truth that petty vengeance, while
   satisfying in the short term, damages both the
   giver and the receiver.

- ***Be kind when providing feedback***

    At the risk of being perceived as too nice, err on the side of being more nurturing and accepting, while striving to provide feedback that is direct, specific, and non-punishing. The goal is not to one-up someone or prove a point, but to encourage self-reflection. If you find with certainty that they have acted in their own best interests to the detriment of others, consider how you can help them contemplate their ill-advised behavior and its related long-term negative consequences. Rather than hold their faults against them, ask them to consider how they could avoid repeating or amplifying their behavior.

- ***Gently remind***

    If they have acknowledged their shortcomings, and are making a sincere effort to modify their behavior, keep a watchful eye for when they slip back into old patterns. Remember that it takes time to shift, so give them some time and remind them without seeming to nag. Also don't show frustration or smugness if they lapse. Perhaps you can both agree upon a secret gesture or catchword to use when they revert back to a behavior that they want to change.

When *you* aren't at your best

We've all made mistakes and done foolish things. We don't set out to be incompetent or insensitive, but there are instances when we let people down, sometimes unknowingly. Imagine being judged for a momentary lapse or weakness, and having that judgment define you for the rest of your life. Even worse, what if it resulted in our losing confidence or led to constant second guessing, or being overly self critical? We need to recognize that we are imperfect beings and as humans we are not infallible. It helps if we can see our mistakes for what they are—mistakes, and not flaws of character.

- *Give yourself time and space to grow*

   Each new job, project, or promotion, comes with the opportunity to develop the knowledge and skills to be successful in something different. Similarly, as we experience new life events, such as starting a relationship, becoming a parent, or moving to a new city, there will be many situations in which settled routines and habits will be challenged by new circumstances and personalities. This period of adaptation may, depending upon your resistance to change and fear of new things, be fraught with mistakes and inadvertent friction. Recognize that we need to give ourselves some wiggle room to be uncomfortable or vulnerable for a while.

- *Do a self-assessment*

   Periodically assess how well you are doing based on what is important to you. In his book, *Triggers: Creating Behavior That Lasts – Becoming the Person You Want to Be*, world-renowned and top-rated executive coach, Dr. Marshall Goldsmith, shares that he asks himself daily *"Did I do my best to...?"* for a number of different aspects in which he cares to become more engaged. [18] He recommends asking questions such as, did I do my best to: set clear goals today; make progress toward my goal today; build positive relationships today; exercise today? If we frequently reinforce our commitment to something, we have a higher chance of staying motivated towards that goal.

- *Ask others to assess you*

  Seek the opinions of others to get an outside perspective of how well you are doing. Accept the positive feedback and compliments with pride and take ownership of addressing the constructive feedback. While it is subjective and you may not agree with some negative views, take the time to internalize what you've heard. Don't be too hasty to dismiss criticism, particularly when it comes from someone you trust and respect, and especially if you solicited it in the first place. Take some time to consider the substance of the critique, as well as its source. You can then make better choices about where you want to focus your attention.

- *Take an assessment*

  There are many assessments available that are designed to be more objective. Assessments can reveal numerous valuable insights to facilitate more self-awareness and self-improvement. Be perfectly candid when answering questions, and you can get a better sense of your personality, characteristics, strengths, blind spots, motivators, values, and general attitude towards life. [19]

Bruce D Schneider, PhD, founder of iPEC Coaching, and author of *Energy Leadership: Transforming Your Workplace and Your Life from the Core* has developed a unique and powerful assessment to quantify our level of energy based on our attitude.[20] The Energy Leadership[TM] Index (E.L.I) is an assessment that helps you to become more aware of what triggers an energy draining reaction in you and what creates an energy boosting behavior.[21] It is an excellent diagnostic tool for assessing the health of your thoughts, feelings, and emotions, much like an EKG assesses the physical health of your heart. Instead of working with a physician, dietician, or personal trainer, you work with a certified coach for a healthier attitude.

- ***Acknowledge without self-criticizing***

  While you don't need to always publicize your mistakes or shortcomings, acknowledging them is the first step towards improvement. Self-assess and self-acknowledge, but don't self-criticize.

  Leaders who assume the burden of knowing everything and being infallible, run the risk of making a bad decision and becoming isolated. By openly acknowledging your motivation, responsibilities, strengths, limitations, and concerns, your family and team can better understand what you are dealing with. Your vulnerability will encourage them to be more transparent and less guarded themselves, creating an atmosphere of open communication.

- *Forgive yourself*

  Do you have a habit of getting angry with yourself after you have made a mistake? Do you replay the situation over and over in your mind? While it is understandable to feel anger and shame, it is unproductive, not to mention unhealthy, to hold onto those emotions for too long. Dwelling on the negative can lead to crippling self-doubt, and the inability to move on. Each new situation will be colored by a bad experience from the past. Forgive yourself, and let go of your ego so that you can move forward. We often judge and reprimand ourselves more harshly than others, and at some point this becomes counterproductive.

- *Take positive action*

  If you are aware of your shortcomings, don't wait for or rely on an external factor or person to make you feel or act differently. Ask for help if needed, but you are ultimately the only person responsible for how you behave and grow. Determine what to do and take positive action.

Good behavior does not negate bad behavior

There are some cases in which you should not provide, or be given, much "Latitude in Your Attitude." Bad behavior needs to be corrected or stopped and it cannot simply be undone by following up with good behavior.

Saying we are sorry is one thing. *Meaning* we are sorry is another. *Not repeating or changing our negative behavior to show we are sorry* is ultimately what is required.

An apology is meaningless unless it is accompanied by modified behavior. There are some who are so accustomed to being on the receiving end of bad behavior, that they are willing to accept the apology at face value, without expecting the necessary change in behavior. Of course, we should not judge others for their reasons for tolerating undesirable interactions. There are many facets of a relationship that we are not privy to, and the complexities of dealing with bad behavior may require professional outside assistance.

If you find yourself needing to apologize for the same behavior more than once, it is time to stop that behavior. You may have heard the joke that if the first person you meet in the morning is a jerk, then you may have met a jerk. If throughout the day you meet a hundred jerks—then you may be the jerk.

In the study *Perpetuating Abusive Supervision: Third Party Reactions to Abuse in the Workplace* led by Jonathan Shaffer, a doctoral student in the UI Tippie College of Business, it was found that third parties tend to accept the abuse if the supervisor is seen to be productive and effective and they do not feel like they are the next target.[22] Previous studies also showed that employees who feel they are abused are less productive, and that organizations that do not specifically have a system in place to assess a supervisor's behavior may be allowing behavior that leads to lower productivity in the long term.

Many are made to feel that they should accept an unhealthy workplace culture; after all, the reasoning goes, they should be lucky they even have a job, albeit in an environment that denigrates and demoralizes.

If bosses are behaving badly at work are they behaving the same way at home with their significant others, parents, children, and siblings?

"There is nothing noble in being superior to your fellow man; true nobility is being superior to your former self."
- Ernest Hemingway

An Attitude of Gratitude

The finest application of having "Latitude in Your Attitude" is when you shift your mindset to one of gratitude. As leaders, when we express or embody gratefulness, we exude and spread a culture of happiness. Perhaps this is only a temporary respite in the context of a significant setback, yet the stopgap may allow us to cultivate a better frame of mind for dealing with an issue.

Ongoing studies on Gratitude and Well-being by Robert Emmons, PhD., show that when we are feeling down or under stress, shifting our thoughts to focus on what we are grateful for can help elevate our mood and our well-being.[23]

We all like to know and hear when we have done something well, not to merely boost our egos, but to get validation that we are doing the right thing and to feel valued and appreciated for doing so.

Expressing appreciation to others

Whether it is for a major accomplishment, a small act of kindness, or a routine daily task, show appreciation to others. It's not the size of the gesture that matters; it's the thoughtfulness of it.

- *Simply say "Thank you"*

  A simple, sincere "Thank you" in the moment goes a long way. If you have the time and especially if you know that someone went to great effort on your behalf, consider sending a "Thank You" card or email.

  Don't take routine tasks for granted. Thanking the person who cooked after each meal, or rang up your purchase, or completed the weekly project status report at work is something we should remember to do. If you feel you are being gratuitous, assess whether you are genuinely thankful. When your manager supports you in a difficult meeting, or your colleague covers for you while you're out, let them know in your next interaction how much you appreciate it.

- *Tailor towards personal preference*
  Not everyone feels appreciated in the same way, so assess whether your expressions of gratitude are truly helping others to feel valued. The book *5 Languages of Appreciation in the Workplace* by Gary Chapman and Paul White, describes the different ways in which we feel appreciated.[24] For example, some of us appreciate words of wisdom more than tangible gifts. We only feel truly encouraged if the message of appreciation is communicated through our primary language.

- *Express in group and 1-on-1 settings*
  If your team worked nights and weekends to meet a tight deadline, a group thank you speech or note to the whole team is needed. If any one particular individual stood out for their contribution, the rest of the team probably saw it too, so be mindful of whether it warrants singling someone out in public, or whether it would be better to let that person know in a 1-on-1, as well as in their review, how much they were appreciated. The risk of applauding someone louder than others may have the effect of demoralizing some on the team who felt they may have contributed just as much but that their contribution was not as easily visible or tangible.

  A well-known example of how *not* to perform team evaluations was given by Microsoft. As reported in a ZDNet, Microsoft announced a fundamental change to their organization.[25] They had earned a notorious reputation for their "Stack Ranking" of employees. For those unfamiliar with this system, all Microsoft employees were graded on a curve that had a pre-targeted distribution. A certain percentage of Microsoft's employees were required to be rated as top performers, good performers, average, and poor.

As you can guess, this fueled a divisive corporate culture that ended up being the topic of an expose published in Vanity Fair.[26] There were tales of infighting and a toxic environment that stifled innovation and led to the development of a siloed organization.

At home, be wary of continually singling out one child's accomplishments at the risk of making the other children in the family look or feel bad and potentially having them feel resentful or less favored. Each child has different strengths and aptitudes. Find the good in each of them and acknowledge it. You can be even handed in your praise without seeming insincere.

Receiving appreciation from others

- ### *Don't be motivated by it*
  It feels good to be complimented for your good deeds, and that endorphin rush can be addictive. However, when you are motivated solely by the need for personal recognition, instead of the value you bring to others, altruism can slip over into narcissism. Take a step back occasionally to question your own motivations. Are you doing it for the good of the project or the group, or simply for the applause? Would

you have done the deed even without receiving recognition? If not, then you are feeding your ego, and not sustaining the group.

- *Gladly accept*

  Sometimes we feel uncomfortable with or undeserving of recognition, not wanting to draw attention to ourselves. When we receive praise, we may have the tendency to deflect, or feel the need to reciprocate, by praising the other person in return. Learn to accept compliments graciously. You deserve it!

- *Use it as an energy boost*

  Praise can give you a physical as well as an emotional boost. So don't just enjoy the moment; take advantage of it as pick-me-up. When we are feeling good about ourselves, we can achieve so much more.

- *Don't rest on your laurels*

  While it is easy and tempting to be content with our past accomplishments and recognition, keep growing. The saying *"What got you here won't get you there"* is a nice reminder.

- *Appreciate private wins*

  Private accomplishments to develop a more positive mindset and new skills can be extremely self-gratifying. Don't minimize your personal triumphs, especially when you are learning to manage your reactions better; for example, if you didn't lose your temper when you might have done so in the past, or when you realized you were being judgmental and paused to assess whether you were making any assumptions. It's okay to give yourself a pat on the back every now and then.

Being grateful

There are some circumstances under which we may find it inconceivable to be grateful, especially when they result in suffering and unfairness. These events are likely to take a toll on our emotional state and physical well-being for a short or extended period of time. There are many ways to work through a tough situation, and as counterintuitive as it may seem, reminding ourselves that there are still aspects in our lives for which to be grateful can lead us to an improved mindset from which to cope and overcome.

Based on a study done by the University of Manchester, a prolonged attitude of gratitude is related to better mood and sleep, less fatigue, and greater satisfaction with life.[27] Cultivating gratitude can broaden our thinking, help us be more optimistic and productive, and increase our desire to help others. In his book *Gratitude Works!: A 21-Day Program for Creating Emotional Prosperity,* Robert A. Emmons writes that gratitude helps us *feel good* and inspires us to *do good*."[28]

- *Make the choice*

  Start by making the conscious choice to be thankful so that you can self-moderate when you are deviating from that option.

- *Make the effort*

  If you want to be happier, make the effort to introduce and stick to a daily gratitude practice of 5-10 minutes for at least three weeks. If you lapse, you can always restart.

- *Start a gratitude journal*

  A gratitude journal can be a physical book or an electronic note in which you write daily. You can even just simply think about what you are grateful for as part of a meditation or mental reflection routine. Each day, I like to think about at least 5 things that I am most grateful for. My family, friends, and health are always on my list, and different items pop up depending on what's happening in my life.

- *Think big, think small, think all*

  There are really no limits to what we can be thankful for. We can be grateful for the Universe in which we live, the people we love, the wonder of our genetic code, the musicians we listen to, the cookie we just ate, or even the toothpaste in our bathroom. If you need help, here's a list on *The Huffington Post on "100 Things To Be Grateful For."*[29]

━━━━━━━━━━━━━━

"At times, our own light goes out and is rekindled by a spark from another person. Each of us has cause to think with deep gratitude of those who have lighted the flame within us."

- Albert Schweitzer

━━━━━━━━━━━━━━

Key Principle and Action

Adopt a more open-minded attitude

By making a conscious shift in your attitude, you can shed old ways of thinking that prevent you from expanding your mind to new and different possibilities. You can choose to be less judgmental by refraining from making assumptions and imposing your personal values on others. You have the opportunity to change your own negative behaviors and to overcome adversity through feelings of gratitude and self-empowerment.

- Become more aware of when you are judging yourself and others based on your own values and beliefs.

- Shift to a more positive mindset of curiosity, acceptance, and shared objectives.

- Don't perpetuate a negative behavior that, in turn, perpetuates a negative environment.

- Be grateful.

Chapter 6
The Elephant in the Room

Popping the last crispy puri bhaji into your mouth, you're appreciative of the culinary experience of a completely different culture. You savor the blend of potatoes, onions, chili, chaat masala, tamarind chutney, and yogurt, before chugging down the rest of your beer. After paying, you head down the crowded street towards a group of young children sitting on the ground, intently listening to an elderly man.

As you watch the man's gestures, it's clear that he is recounting the story of "The Blind Men and the Elephant" in which six blind men were asked to figure out what an elephant looked like by feeling different parts of the elephant's body. The man who feels a leg says the elephant is like a pillar; the one who feels the tail says the elephant is like a rope; the one who feels the trunk says the elephant is like a tree branch; the one who feels the ear says the elephant is like a hand fan; the one who feels the belly says the elephant is like a wall; and the one who feels the tusk says the elephant is like a solid pipe. All of them were right and wrong at the same time since the elephant is the sum of its very different parts. Only by putting them all together, could they really understand what an elephant is.

Before the story is over, the mobile phone you bought at the start of your trip to India rings. The sound of your colleague's voice from several time zones away doesn't surprise you. It was only a matter of time before someone on the team finally spoke up about the very visible elephant in the room.

The Elephant in the Room

Much like having the different perspectives of the helicopter and the Humvee®, the parable of the "The Blind Men and the Elephant" teaches the importance of getting the big picture before forming an opinion.

Unlike the story of "The Blind Men and the Elephant" where the men lacked the visual perception to see what was in front of them, the elephant in the room is highly visible. It is an important, obvious, and uncomfortable truth about a problematic person or situation that is often left unaddressed, even though everyone is aware of the problem.

It's important to address a problematic situation with clarity and calmness before it leads to greater issues.

Ignoring the Elephant

There are many reasons for choosing to ignore or sidestep the elephant. However, failing to acknowledge and address it may lead to even greater issues down the road. It's important to consider why we tolerate the elephant and whether we should continue to do so.

Dealing with the Elephant

Once we decide to deal with the elephant, we should do so thoughtfully and deliberately. The intention is to improve a situation and not to embarrass or belittle others.

"When there's an elephant in the room, introduce him."

- Randy Pausch

Ignoring the Elephant

Unless you are Blake Dinkin who is making the world's most expensive and unique elephant dung coffee, an elephant doesn't belong in your office. The Canadian entrepreneur waits for elephants to relieve themselves of the coffee beans they have been fed in the jungles of Thailand's Golden Triangle. He cleans and roasts the beans that have undergone a transformation during their passage through the elephant's digestive system to produce a coffee that is described as rich, smooth, and nutty. Even if you wanted to try Mr. Dinkin's exclusive Black Ivory Coffee at home, you certainly don't need to keep an elephant in the kitchen.[30]

Reasons we ignore or tolerate it

So why do we ignore or tolerate the Elephant in the Room?

- *It's too sensitive*

  Even though an elephant is hardly delicate, uncomfortable truths are extremely difficult and oftentimes tricky to deal with. For example: an inexperienced manager who leads the team astray or fails to lead at all; an individual who lacks key skills to get the job done; an unrealistic timeline for a project; or an impossible goal to accomplish. Examples on a more serious personal note include: someone who is dealing with and not confronting emotional, physical, or sexual abuse, substance abuse, mental illness, or infidelity.

- *It's just a baby elephant*

  The issue at hand appears small and trivial, but like a baby elephant, it has the potential to grow very large, even large enough to crowd out all other issues. If we can address the matter in its infancy it will be much easier to tackle.

- *It's too big to deal with*

  Once the situation in question is acknowledged, there is still the responsibility of handling it. In some cases, the perception may be that it will take more time and energy than ignoring it. We may also feel that we lack the courage or the ability to deal with it. On one end of the spectrum of possible solutions, the issue could be handled by a one-on-one discussion with the right person; on the other end, it might require the support of a professional team or the entire extended family. Sometimes, addressing it makes the situation far worse before it gets better.

- *It could have undesirable consequences*

  Even if you start with the best intentions when deciding to deal with the elephant, the desired outcome might not be achieved. Instead of being given the opportunity to be coached or re-assigned to a more suitable role, a valued employee could lose their job. A family may have to be split up or more cover-ups could be devised. If not handled correctly, it has the potential to be unnecessarily embarrassing and distressing to innocent bystanders. There is also the possibility of retribution for those raising the issue.

  Once you say something, it is almost impossible to take it back, so we may fear hurting feelings, damaging relationships, or some kind of retaliation.

- ***It won't make a difference***

  It could be that we are resigned to having the elephant in the room because we believe that no course of action will change the situation. We aren't prepared to spend the time and energy on a seemingly futile effort. Sometimes office politics are a more powerful force than even the largest elephant.

- ***It's in our blind spot***

  While some choose to turn a blind eye, others may truly have a blind spot or be in total denial that an issue exists.

- ***It's in the room next door***

  When an issue doesn't directly impact us, we may be inclined to leave well enough alone if we are not directly impacted, or no one is in a life-threatening situation or breaking the law. However, let us not forget that elephants can walk from room to room, or that some people find they can deal with the elephant in their room by subtly directing it to yours!

The Elephant and the Emperor

As mentioned before, an elephant in the room is an important and obvious truth that everyone is aware of but is reluctant to discuss because it is uncomfortable and is therefore, often left unaddressed.

In the Danish fairy tale *The Emperor's New Clothes* written by Hans Christian Andersen and first published in 1837, we see how a vain Emperor is swindled by two tailors and fooled into marching in a procession wearing only his underwear. They promise him a fine suit made from fabric invisible to any wearer who is unfit for his position. Although the Emperor cannot see the fabric himself, neither he nor his ministers will admit it. During the procession, his subjects, fearful of repercussions, play along with the pretense, except for a child too young to understand. The little boy shouts out that the Emperor has no clothes and the crowd, now emboldened, follows suit. The Emperor realizes the foolishness of his vanity and decides to take his position more seriously in the future. Put yourself in the Emperor's shoes (well, he was at least wearing those), and ask yourself if you want to live a pretense. If you'd rather have the (ahem) naked truth, there are far less embarrassing ways to uncover it.

We also need the wisdom to recognize that in some cases, simply verbalizing that there is an elephant in the room may be all we can do. There are many reasons for a decision to not address it directly or immediately. However, to ensure the situation does not get out of control, consider everyone who might be impacted and what they will each need to cope with the situation. Living with and adapting to or tolerating a situation will be different for each person.

Dealing with the Elephant

Acknowledging there is an elephant in the room is the first critical step, but it won't go away by itself. A plan needs to be formulated and since the male African elephant is the largest living land animal and can weigh nearly 7 tons, moving it may be challenging. For animal conservationists who move elephants to safer locations, the well-being and security of the animal is of the utmost concern. Similarly, dealing with the elephant in the room will require sensitivity to those concerned so as not to embarrass anyone or trigger any negative consequences. Communicate that the intent is to be helpful rather than hurtful.

When deciding to address the elephant, keep the bigger picture in mind, as every action taken to address a situation will have one or more repercussions, some positive, some not. Playing out possible scenarios *before confronting the elephant* may be necessary to help understand and anticipate various potential outcomes. If a win/win is not possible, understand what compromises can be made in the interest of all, showing respect and consideration for those concerned.

If you are *raising* the issue...

- ***Is the issue directly impacting you?***
  When a situation is having a negative impact on you personally, as difficult as it may be, making the decision to raise awareness is the first big step. If necessary, find confidants who can help

provide an objective assessment and support you through the process. Perhaps you will find allies in those who are also affected.

- *Are you informed?*

    If you are not directly impacted, it is important to have a good sense of what the uncomfortable truth really is. Understanding the issue, the current impacts, and the future implications will help in assessing the scope and critical degree of the issue so that it can be appropriately dealt with. When gathering information, consider the privacy and respect of those involved. Try to get various perspectives and avoid jumping to conclusions too soon.

- *Do you know who to reach out to?*

    A confidante could be a trusted colleague, family member, or friend, or it could also be an external professional or family matter support group. Determine who can best help address the issue. Assess whether to seek assistance from a relative, a friend, a manager, a human resources contact, a trained professional, or perhaps even the person at the core of the issue.

- *Can you effectively articulate the issue?*

    Once you have a good grasp on the situation, prepare to clearly, objectively, and calmly articulate it. If you are confronting the elephant directly, approach with caution and tact. Share that you want to provide some feedback, and that you are also interested in hearing his or her perspective. Cultivate the demeanor of an advisor rather than a prosecutor.

- ***Are you prepared for the immediate reaction?***

  If the person who is the elephant immediately reacts with denial or anger, acknowledge what they are saying and that it is understandable for them to feel that way. Remain calm and give them time to process what they have just heard. If necessary, tell them you will follow-up with them at a later time. Depending on the situation, it may be difficult to control your own emotions, so also take some time to compose yourself before continuing.

- ***Are you prepared to deal with the final outcome?***

  Assuming that raising the issue will result in some follow-up, ensure that you are aware of, and are prepared to deal with, the possible outcomes and unintended consequences. In the best case, the elephant is acknowledged and dealt with tactfully and properly. In the worst case, you might need to deal with retaliation or a worsening situation. Assess whether you will have a support system if needed.

If you are in a position to *help address* the issue...

- ***Are you visible?***

  Make sure people are aware that you are someone they can reach out to. Communicate that in your role in the organization, the family, or the community, you are expected and/or willing to be someone who can help facilitate a resolution.

If the elephant is in someone else's room and you are asked to help, be sensitive to whether it is appropriate and to the fact that you might not have the full picture. Assist with humility rather than seeing yourself as the hero.

If it is part of the responsibility of your role, don't hide behind the elephant because you don't want to deal with it. If you don't feel up to it, let them know where they may find help instead.

- ***Are you available?***

  When someone finally builds up the courage to approach a taboo subject, make yourself available to discuss it with them. As a manager/individual contributor, parent/child, or part of any group, it is important to be physically, intellectually, and emotionally accessible to those relying on you. There is little value in having an open door policy if you are never there.

- ***Are you approachable?***

  Even after you've cleared your calendar and mind for a conversation, set the tone for productive dialogue. Do what you can to put the person at ease during what will likely be a difficult and uncomfortable discussion. Listen and ask questions to understand and try not to be judgmental or jump to conclusions that cause someone to become defensive.

- *Are you going to follow-up?*

  Depending on the circumstance, you may decide to coach the individual on how to handle the situation themselves, to refer them to someone else, to personally deal with it, or to escalate to someone who is in a better position to help. Communicate your decision and the rationale behind it so they leave knowing the discussion was worthwhile.

  Discretely follow-up with others from whom you can learn more details or who can resolve the issue. Also keep the person who brought the issue to your attention informed of progress or obstacles. It might be necessary for them to take specific actions or change their own behaviors to help solve the problem.

- *Are you going to cover it up?*

  If you are associated with or benefitting from the elephant in the room and you decide to cover it up, push it aside, or feed it, you may end up being the second elephant in the room.

If *you* are "the elephant"...

- *Are you aware?*

  Take the time for self-reflection on a regular basis to assess how your words and actions may be affecting those around you. Seek feedback from people at work and at home who will provide candid responses based on your desire to make improvements.

- *Will you listen calmly?*

  When it is brought to our attention that we may be the center of an issue, understandably our first reaction might be to act defensively. We may experience feelings of embarrassment, confusion, anger, resentment, or denial. It may be difficult to manage our immediate instinct to make counter arguments and go on the offensive. Take some quiet time to reflect to minimize the risk of rejecting or alienating those who care about us the most.

- *Will you shoot the messenger?*

  We must also recognize that it wasn't easy for the messenger to bring such an uncomfortable and personal topic to our attention. Don't resent them or damage your relationship with them.

- *Will you be appreciative?*

  Hopefully, you will see that they have your best interest at heart. Acknowledge how difficult it must have been to broach the topic, and express your gratitude. You might even feel a sense of relief that something you may have been privately suffering with is now out in the open.

- *Are you afraid?*

  Perhaps you are in the room because you really are afraid of the alternative. Keeping the status quo may feel easier or more comfortable than making a move. Ask yourself what is behind your fears and how you might be able to overcome them.

- *Are you able to move on your own?*

  There may be obstacles to leaving the room that prevent you from doing so on your own. Find someone with whom you can confide and who can help you to get the support, resources, or courage to take the necessary steps.

- *Are you willing to take responsibility?*

  Ideally, we need to internalize what we have become aware of, and assess our appropriate response. We can take responsibility for making a change and taking positive action. We might be able to swiftly resolve the issue on our own, or we might face a long, arduous journey with support from many others. Remind yourself that while you may leave as the unwanted elephant, you have the opportunity to return with a whole new, more positive persona.

Key Principle and Action

Handle uncomfortable truths calmly and respectfully

If you don't acknowledge and address a problematic person or situation, it may lead to even greater issues down the road. If you are raising the issue, helping to address the issue, or the focus of the issue, you will need to approach the situation with clarity and calmness.

- Provide an environment that encourages open discussion of important and oftentimes uncomfortable topics.

- Develop your skills in resolving challenging situations for a positive outcome.

- Be open to taking positive action if you are the issue.

Chapter 7
Oil and Vinegar are Better Together

Without doubt, the most frequent question asked in our family is "What's for dinner?" With so many options and favorites, it's always difficult to decide. But, if we go for Peruvian cuisine, I have a ready answer. It's always Lomo Saltado.

The first time I ordered it, I found it unusual that this flavorful dish has French fries mixed into the rice, along with soy sauce marinated strips of steak, onions, and tomatoes. I've since learned it is representative of a fusion of Cantonese and Peruvian flavors which originated during the influx of Chinese immigrants to Peru in the late 19th and 20th Century.

"Chifa" cuisine, as it became known, originates from Cantonese and means "to eat rice" or "to have a meal." Arroz chaufa is another chifa dish. Chaufa comes from the Cantonese word for "fried rice." Other dishes include Wantan frito (or fried wonton) and pollo enrollado (chicken rolled into fried crust). In fact, Chifa is so deeply integrated with Peruvian food, that it has become regarded as authentically Peruvian.

Not all fusion cuisine becomes imbedded into a single culture, but there are many interesting combinations, and creative chefs continue to innovate. In culinary capitals of the world, there are Asian-Italian hybrids (Orsa and Winston, Los Angeles) as well as Jewish-Japanese (Shalom Japan, New York) and Mexican-Korean (Kogi BBQ, Los Angeles). These are culture clashes that everyone can appreciate.

Oil and Vinegar are Better Together

As any cook can tell you, oil and vinegar just don't mix. Force them together by vigorously mixing them up, and within a short time, they will settle back into distinct layers with the heavier oil on the bottom and the lighter vinegar on top.

Because oil is hydrophobic (water-fearing) and vinegar is hydrophilic (water-loving), they will eventually separate, no matter how hard we shake them together. For oil and vinegar to stay mixed, we need to add an emulsifier. Emulsifiers have both hydrophobic and hydrophilic regions, so they can pull the oil and vinegar together to create an emulsion. Some emulsifiers also act as stabilizers.

So why force two things together when they are so clearly antagonistic to each other? Well because sometimes, they are actually great together. A basic vinaigrette with just oil, vinegar, salt and pepper, can be exceptional depending on the quality of the ingredients. If made ahead or in bulk, the separated dressing will need to be shaken up again prior to serving. Fortunately, the effort of making a homemade dressing will be rewarded by the result. The proof of the pudding (or in this case salad), as they say, is in the tasting.

Adding herbs and spices can further enhance the taste. We can also add a selection of other ingredients like mustard, honey, garlic paste, egg, or dairy products, to create more complex dressings such as honey-mustard, aioli, Caesar, and sesame ginger. These ingredients all have the extra benefit of being emulsifiers and/or stabilizers. The endless possibilities of unique and flavorful gastronomic fusions are what a foodie's dreams are made of!

So, what does the science and variety of salad dressing have to do with leadership concepts, you ask? It is analogous to the chemistry of relationships within diverse teams and households; and the richness of thought and outcome because of these relationships.

Blended households and teams

Each family, household, or organization is a blended entity in which individuals are constantly interacting.

As an ingredient

Each of us, with our distinct backgrounds and talents, adds a different element to the mix. How we show up in that mix can enhance or spoil it.

As an emulsifier or stabilizer

Just like food ingredients, not all individuals integrate well naturally and we may need to apply extra effort to reap the benefits of their association. On occasion, our role will be to act as an emulsifier or stabilizer.

As a chef

At times, being a leader, requires us to take the role of the executive chef who must mold talented, yet fractious individuals into a cohesive team or blended household. And like the most inspired chefs, we come up with combinations of ingredients never before considered (like salt and caramel, or bacon and chocolate).

As a vessel

Vessels are the communities in which blending takes place. Some are more conducive to promoting and supporting great blends while others allow toxicity to seep in and spread.

"According to the Spanish proverb, four persons are wanted to make a good salad: a spendthrift for oil, a miser for vinegar, a counselor for salt, and a madman to stir it all up."
- *John Gerard*

Blended households and teams

Every family or household is a blended entity, and every organization is a blended association. Individuals in households and organizations may have similar or different ethnic backgrounds, financial means, educational opportunities, life experiences, personalities, physical attributes, or interests.

Each blend is ever changing, not only because individuals enter or leave the mix over time, but also because individuals themselves are constantly changing. They may even bring something different to each mix in which they find themselves.

There is always an adjustment period as the individuals get to know each other. Sometimes the assimilation is quick and easy, and sometimes it is awkward and can take longer. If there are strong cultural or personality differences, there may even be some resistance or tension.

Ideally, we can all recognize, appreciate, value, leverage, and learn from the qualities of all the individuals. Team or family ties are enhanced when individual's strengths can be combined. Similarly, assisting members to overcome their weaknesses without harsh and accusatory judgment, leads to a more cohesive and appreciative (and therefore loyal) organization.

As an ingredient

Walk into any gourmet grocery store and you will be astonished by the variety and flavor of both oil and vinegar. Like fine wines, olive oils are differentiated by region, by vintage and by variety. On top of that, they may be infused with flavors, such as garlic, rosemary, citrus, and bacon. Aged balsamic vinegars may also be flavored with ingredients such as fig, dark chocolate, and Serrano pepper honey.

Similarly, as team members, we are each complex beings, with our own unique ancestry, character and personal histories. We bring distinct qualities to any relationship or group and we continue to enrich ourselves as we interact with others.

- *Be proud of your heritage*
  We inherit much, simply based on our birth; and our heritage is further augmented by the customs or traditions adopted by our families and communities. The person you are now is the culmination of all your experiences and

influences. No one else has had the totality of your experiences, or encountered them in exactly the same way. Resist the impulse to make apologies to your group about perceived failings that may be attributable to non-conforming cultural or regional differences.

- *Learn about others*

  Unless you live in an isolation chamber, far from humans of any description, you will realize that it is increasingly a diverse and multicultural world. If you are going to be interacting with others in a professional, personal, or social capacity, it is incumbent upon you to get to know them better. Seek to understand what is important to them and how they prefer to interact. Be mindful of differing cultural norms and communicate in a way that is appropriate and respectful. After all, would you not appreciate the same effort from others?

- *Enrich yourself*

  Approach each new situation as a learning experience. A simple curious conversation can uncover a treasure trove of someone else's experiences. Be careful not to pry, though! Multiply that by the number of people you interact with and the rewards can be infinite.

  When you leave your comfort zone inside a given group, you can find many avenues to learn new skills and gain knowledge. Try to experience new things whenever you can. By enriching yourself, you enrich your community.

- *Enrich your community*

  Share information and your experience with others. Adopt a mindset of collaboration instead of competition. Of course, some competition is healthy and can stimulate growth and new ideas, but when it crosses the line into a cutthroat survival of the fittest, the inevitable endpoint is that the few will win at the expense of the many. In this case, competition itself can be the problem's cause and not its solution.

  Everyone has something to contribute to a group, be it a fresh look, or a new idea, or just a different perspective on an old problem.

- *Right size your contribution*

  Sometimes you may be the entree, and at others, the accompaniment to support and enhance the main dish. Learn to be comfortable in either role. Being the most senior, knowledgeable, or voluble person, does not necessarily mean your contribution is the most important. Don't impose your will on other constituents within the group. Calibrate the level and tone of your contributions and give others the chance to speak up.

  On the other hand, if you feel you have something to offer, and are not given the opportunity to express it, don't be afraid to interject in a polite and respectful way. Do not let your reticence deprive the group of the benefit of your insight.

- *Experience a different mix*

  The connections we make throughout our lives never disappear. They may fade, become dormant, or less frequent, as we grow and move on. Or, they may become stronger and richer. Think of the friends you knew in high school. Some are close friends to this day. Others you can barely recall. We connect with those who are right for us at a particular time in our development, and some we keep for life. But it is also possible that some connections are toxic, or stunt our growth. It could be as dangerous as a gang, or as innocuous as a codependent friendship. But both prevent us from making new and beneficial relationships, by keeping us trapped in a stagnant mindset.

  Find ways to broaden your interests or contribute to different groups. You might find them to be as appreciative of you as you are of them.

- *Don't spoil the mix*

  Have you ever made a cup of coffee and when you pour in the milk, you find the milk is spoiled? Nothing ruins a fresh cup of coffee like spoiled milk. Don't be that milk! If you are having a negative impact on those around you, and you have been made aware of this, take the necessary steps to modify your behavior. Your initial instinct might be to deflect, or blame others, rather than to take responsibility. Of course, it is never easy to be confronted with your own shortcomings. If necessary, don't be afraid to reach out for help if you are unable to work through a behavioral shift on your own.

- ### *Leave a mix*

  If you find that you are in a team or organization that does not bring out the best in you, first assess if you are bringing out the best in yourself. Perhaps your skills need an upgrade, or your attitude needs adjustment. However, if you believe you are in an environment that no longer supports your core values or your purpose for being in the group, find a different one. Don't hang around for too long if you find that you're becoming increasingly unhappy. You may be reluctant to leave if you believe you are a key ingredient, an emulsifier, or a chef, but the environment and you will be better off in the long run. No individual is truly indispensable. Another ingredient will be found.

  Having said that, it is not always easy, or even possible to simply leave, especially in family situations. Assess how you can become a better ingredient or emulsifier and consider leaving as a last resort. If leaving is not an option, then you must work on ways to coexist without tension, or to limit your interaction to minimize conflicts.

As an emulsifier or stabilizer

Emulsifiers and stabilizers have a role in creating a stable mixture. They come in many forms from egg yolks to mustard to dairy products. Similarly, what holds blended groups together comes in many forms and we can all be emulsifiers.

- *Establish core values*

  I believe the most effective emulsifier for a functional household or team is a shared set of core values. These need to be established early and reinforced often. Core values are like the sturdy framework of a building, or the keystone of an arch. Without them, no matter how elaborate the facade or fancy the additions, the whole structure is susceptible to the slightest internal or external stress.

  For example, does an organization truly value openness and honesty, or is it comfortable with dissimulation when it is convenient or expedient? Do the executives abide by their expressed values, or are they really driven by the bottom line?

  Family dynamics are fraught with conflicting values. In a household with mixed religions, how is the child to be brought up? Does parental support extend beyond adulthood, or are the children expected to fend for themselves at an arbitrary age?

  So many problems can be avoided if there is an agreement on what factors should drive the decisions. Of course, you cannot provide for every eventuality, but if there is consensus on the values that frame the problematic situation, it can limit the potentially destructive nature of conflicts that go to the very root of organizational beliefs.

- ***Respect differences in core values***

  Internal and external conflict arises when competing values are incompatible, especially if the opposing parties consider those values non-negotiable. While I am not advocating the slippery slope of moral relativity, I would point out that extreme rigidity is fatal to cooperation. To avoid instability, parties should discuss acceptable compromises as soon as a potential conflict is identified, rather than ignoring the problem until it is too big to ignore (see the Elephant in the Room).

- ***Model core values***

  Not all values have to be explicitly stated and enumerated. This could lead to a contract only a transactional attorney could love. Some values flow naturally from observable actions and the way in which we express ourselves in certain situations. Employees take their cues from their bosses. Team members look to their manager to set the tone. Children model their behavior on their parents. Whether explicit or implicit, the values that you exhibit have consequences. You cannot expect others to honor your values, if you do not live by them yourself. "Do what I say, and not what I do" is the mantra of a corrupt autocracy and not a formula for respect.

- *Respect differences in behavior*

  As previously stated, in diverse or global households and organizations, there will be cultural differences. Learn about these differences and tailor your interactions accordingly.

- *Enhance your communication skills*

  We all have the ability to be the glue that binds our group together. Effective communication is an essential skill in achieving that cohesiveness. Learn to look out for the many small interactions that tend to either enhance group dynamics, or alienate team members. Without jumping to conclusions, try to pick up on what is not being said, and validate that you have assessed the underlying values and emotions accurately. Communicate with others in your group to create stronger connections. Facilitate or engage in productive conversations to resolve conflict. Communication is more than a mere exchange of words. To truly communicate, you have to learn to actively listen when the other person is speaking.

- *Include everyone*

  Inclusiveness is vital to cohesion within a group. Exclusion leads to resentment, suspicion, and ultimately to a breakdown of the group dynamic. That pinch of salt in the dressing may not contribute much by way of volume, but if the emulsifier cannot incorporate it, the salad will be poorer for it.

- ***Allow inactive elements***

  Some medications contain inactive ingredients. Why would they be included if they don't appear to have any pharmacological or therapeutic effect? The answer is that they often combine with active ingredients to facilitate drug transport in the body. Sometimes, they are binding agents, or add flavor or color to otherwise unpalatable medicines.

  In a team or organization, not everyone needs to be active at the same level at all times. There will be situations where it is appropriate and even effective for some members to step back and have a more passive or dormant role. For instance, the marketing team, having done their part to promote the product, may have a reduced role now that the sales force moves into high gear. They are not in any way less important to the functioning of the team. There may be times when you could be the inactive element, so enjoy the opportunity to observe and learn. Your time will come again.

"A Béarnaise sauce is simply an egg yolk, a shallot, a little tarragon, vinegar, and butter, but it takes years of practice for the result to be perfect."

- Fernand Point

As a chef

As a chef, you are responsible for coming up with the recipe, and determining how to create a dressing with a multitude of ingredients. Some ingredients were inherited, some were given to you, some were personally selected by you, and some were even made by you. When you are the head of a household or team, you have the role of a chef.

Most inspired chefs can create a multitude of dishes with any ingredients at hand. However, even the best chefs can stumble, and there may be cases where, no matter how much effort or creativity is applied, two ingredients are simply unable to happily coexist. In these cases, it might be better to use those ingredients in a different recipe, or to find those individuals areas where their unique talents may be best utilized.

- *Collaborate with your team*

  As the only chef or part of a team of chefs, you will need to establish your shared objectives. In co-parenting and co-management positions, without a coordinated and cohesive view of what you would like to accomplish, you could end up with an unpalatable mishmash. Without a clear vision and a plan for execution, your household or team will be confused and may find themselves seeking direction from one lead at the expense of the other. They may even learn to play one against the other to advance their own agenda, since there is no clear direction.

- ***Have a communicated vision***

  With years of training and experience, some
  chefs can simply throw ingredients together and
  come up with something amazing. At least that
  is what it looks like to a casual observer. The
  truth is that the best chefs begin with an idea of
  what they are trying to achieve, and apply their
  deep knowledge of ingredients and processes to
  create their piece de resistance. It only looks like
  they are throwing things together to see what
  sticks, ending up with a masterpiece as if by
  magic or pure luck. The cooks on the line,
  entrusted to bringing the chef's concept to life,
  can only do so if they trust the chef's vision,
  because it has been communicated to them
  clearly and effectively, and each person knows
  their part and what is expected of them.

- ***Know your ingredients***

  Chefs know their ingredients. They would not
  add salt when a recipe called for sugar.
  Similarly, they would not use a cleaver when a
  paring knife would do. Know your ingredients.
  Use the right tool for the right job.

  Get to know the members of your group
  well, especially if you are new to them. Once
  you are familiar with them, place them in
  situations in which they can play to their
  strengths. But remember that the way ingredients
  interact may change depending on the recipe; so
  be aware of their nuances, adaptability, and
  potential incompatibility under different
  circumstances.

- *Evolve or create new recipes*

  There are very few, if any, single use ingredients in a kitchen. A chef will use tomatoes in a pasta sauce, but also in salads, soups and gravies. Keep exploring how you can improve your blend with the same or new ingredients. You may have two talented team members who, for one reason or another, simply do not complement each other well in the same project or team. Determine how you can utilize them in different ways or on different projects.

- *Shake things up*

  When it feels like you are serving up the same old tired dish, shake things up. A chef may use edible flowers as a garnish instead of parsley, instantly transforming an old favorite into something fresh and exciting. Without the willingness to experiment, we can become complacent or bored, which affects our level of engagement and ultimately, our productivity and effectiveness. Do not let your team fall into a comfortable, yet boring routine. Too much change, especially if implemented rapidly and in an arbitrary manner, can be disruptive and unsettling and can lead to low morale, but positive change can be an effective agent for growth and fulfillment.

- *Use helpful tools and techniques*

  Although chefs still rely on old methods and tools, the most innovative are not afraid to embrace new technologies and gadgets that make their job easier, or give them more options. There is an entire new wave of chefs who have adopted techniques of molecular gastronomy, which marries cutting edge science with culinary arts, and has given us a new way of experiencing food.

Never stop learning. Explore new ways to make more cohesive blends—take classes, read, watch, and experiment. Continue to enhance your communication skills. The rules of leadership are not set in stone. The way we lead across generations, borders, and technological advances keeps changing and so should we.

- *Improvise*

  Rarely do we have everything that we need, and even when we do, something happens and we find ourselves floundering. In engineering, they call it Murphy's Law - if anything can go wrong, it will. In a professional kitchen, this is known as being "in the weeds" which means that the cooks are being overwhelmed and are falling behind. Instead of becoming flustered or frozen by indecision, figure out how to improvise. The best cooks do it all the time. Very often, solutions that start off as a temporary fix can evolve to become an integral part of the team or process.

As a vessel

You need a bowl or a jar to mix your dressing, and a container to serve it from. Organizations, communities, households, and families are the vessels in which the blending of teams and individuals takes place and in which the final mix is stored.

Teams need leaders and organizations not only to promote the importance of diversity, but also to provide the resources and support to implement it in order to effect real progress.

Individuals need their communities and families to promote and embody diversity in all its forms. A vessel needs to be both strong and transparent to accommodate the valuable ingredients that have been blended together.

"We may have all come on different ships, but we're in the same boat now."
- Martin Luther King, Jr.

Key Principle and Action

Respect and incorporate diversity

It takes time and effort to bring and keep seemingly disparate individuals together, but a blended group is far more enriched and enriching than a homogenous one. Each of us has a role to play as part of the multiple ever-changing blends to which we belong, now and in the future.

- Embrace your heritage.

- Learn about and experience other cultures.

- Offer your unique contributions to a group, thereby enriching it. Encourage others to do the same.

- Seek to bring diverse perspectives together.

Chapter 8
Do It With Soul

In the 1960's, soul music dominated the R&B charts, with hits like "Respect" by Aretha Franklin, and "A Change is Gonna Come" by Sam Cooke. But what is "soul?" If you're talking about music, it is a vocal style filled with feeling, straight out of the gospel tradition of Southern Black churches. When it began, it wasn't polished, or dressed up. It wasn't just about technical artistry and sweet harmonies. No, it was raw and emotional and based on personal testimony. Soul is the awakening of the spirit, an affirmation of

*the deepest, grandest part of the self, the part of you
that makes you feel what it is to be truly alive.*

*"Dancin' in the Street," by Martha and the
Vandellas brings to mind people cavorting joyfully
while a fire hydrant sprays water in the street. But
whether intentionally or not, it also became an
anthem for societal upheaval in the 60's. The call to
people to come together around the world and take to
the streets, inspired youth, women and people of
color to come out and demand change, find deeper
meaning and transform society—by doing it with
soul.*

Do It With Soul

Findings in Gallup's *State of the American
Workplace* report for 2017 show that only 33% of
employees in the United States are engaged at work,
compared to 70% of employees in the world's best
organizations. [31] Data was collected from over
195,600 U.S. employees and over 31 million
respondents. 51% of employees are not engaged and
simply going through the motions at work, and 16%
are actively disengaged, using their misery to
undermine the impact of the actively engaged group.
In the report, Gallup's recommendations include
changing the culture to that of purpose and coaching,
and transforming managers and leaders at all levels.
Employees are more motivated by meaningful and
challenging work, and positive working
environments.

While no one has commissioned a similar *Study of the American Family* report, there are obvious analogies. The parallel in households is that some members interact with each other in meaningful and uplifting ways, others co-exist in an arrangement of convenience or mutual tolerance, and the rest are causing rifts due to their own unhappiness. Fortunately, we have a lot more control over what motivates a higher level of engagement within our families than we might have professionally. Although we rarely talk about disengagement at home, the concept still exists.

In fact, whether at work or at home, we are all likely to fluctuate from actively engaged, to actively disengaged, depending on the situation. Keeping actively engaged in both environments requires us to put our heart and soul into an activity or a relationship. This is far easier to do when what we are doing, and with whom we are interacting, resonate with us on a personal level. When we can play to our natural strengths, we are inclined to feel more at ease, and are more productive, irrespective of how trivial or challenging the activity. This leads us to feeling more fulfilled, which improves the workplace or family, simply because happiness and goodwill is contagious.

So unless we want to be disengaged from life and those around us, whatever we do, we should "Do It With Soul."

Doing It *Without* Soul

We're not always aware of when we're "Doing It *Without* Soul." Over time, we can become really good at something and we continue to do it without realizing that we're no longer deriving passion or meaning from doing it.

Soul-searching

Some soul-searching can help you to understand whether where you're spending the most of your time and energy is aligned with your personal and family goals.

Doing It *With* Soul

When we're "Doing it with soul," we're deriving pleasure from even the most mundane to the most exciting activities.

Feeding the Soul

Like any living organism, we need to feed our soul in order to thrive and experience the joy of dancing in the street!

One person with passion is better than forty people merely interested."
— *E. M. Forster*

Doing It *Without* Soul

At its extreme, "Doing It *Without* Soul" is akin to mindlessly following a predetermined process without thought or enthusiasm. There are certainly some activities that are purely mechanical or routine, but if we approach them with a robotic mindset, the tedium will eventually infect our contentment, and boredom will turn into resentment.

This was highlighted for me when we first moved to the United States. In South Africa, most of the household chores were taken care of by our live-in nanny and later, by her daughter. After we emigrated, all of those chores—the cooking, the cleaning, the laundry, and dozens of other tasks we had taken for granted—became our responsibility. I quickly realized that housework is fairly low on my list of favorite things. Well, I rolled up my sleeves and did it, but I was resentful, and grumbled every minute that I wiped and dusted and cleaned. It came to a head one day when my husband, who was mopping alongside me, turned and said, "Look, this is something we have to do whether we like it or not. So either do it, or don't do it. But don't do it if you're going to bitch and moan the whole time. It just makes the whole job unpleasant." My first reaction was embarrassment, which later turned to appreciation. I would still much rather be doing something else, but when I need to do my share of keeping our home clean and organized, I have since developed a different demeanor. I have to admit that I still need to psych myself up for it, but I value having a clean and uncluttered environment. I now put myself into a zone by listening to (soul) music or a podcast, and appreciating that I actually have a home to clean. Seeing the end result is always a pleasure. The strange thing is that I enjoy washing dishes—I find it oddly therapeutic. The daily routine of washing and rinsing becomes a ritual and puts me in a meditative state that approaches a Zen-like calmness.

Not all repetitive tasks are mechanical or routine. Sometimes, "Doing It *Without* Soul" happens when the malaise creeps up on us surreptitiously. We are oblivious to the fact that we continue to do something that no longer feeds our soul. Perhaps over time, we become really good at something. We may even be highly valued or sought out for our expertise. But, what we do not realize is that *being* good at something is no longer *doing* us good. Time passes, and the 10 years of experience turns into experiencing the same year 10 times. Ask yourself whether you have any regrets today and whether you might have regrets in the future.

Thankfully, even though we may temporarily lose our way, there are ways to lead us back to where we can "Do It With Soul."

Soul-searching

If we strive to "Do It With Soul," a good place to start is with some soul-searching. We can analyze what drives us and decide whether our goals or visions are aligned with what we are doing.

- *Understand what drives you*

  You would think you know yourself quite well. You might be surprised. Over the course of my career, I have taken various personality assessments. They were helpful in understanding how I liked to approach my work and how to interact with colleagues who had a different style to mine. But I could not pinpoint or clearly articulate why I absolutely loved doing certain activities, tolerated some, and only begrudgingly did others, until I took a test designed to evaluate what corporate culture I would fit well in, and what type of roles would be optimal for me. It proved to be a revelation, and liberated me from preconceptions and expectations I had previously held. More importantly, it further fueled my courage and commitment to help others focus on doing more of what they love, and on spending time with people that lift their spirits.

  You may intuitively know what drives you, but I would encourage you to conduct a thorough self-analysis and make a comprehensive list of what you absolutely love to do, what you are okay with, and what you detest. The list could include aspects related to your career, your role, or even your hobbies.

  If you have not already done so, you may even want to invest in taking one of the many assessments available that give deeper insight into your natural inclinations. Just as we would not invest our hard-earned money in the stock market without doing some research, so too ought we to embark on a voyage of self-discovery before further investing in our next venture.

• *Say no*

Learn to say no to anything you believe you would not enjoy after doing it for some time. If you are unsure, try it for a while. You might find you had a limiting belief about yourself or made assumptions about the role. It might also lead to another role that you enjoy more.

With the knowledge I have gained from both self-reflection and various assessments, I am much clearer about specific values, motivators, and preferences that are my own drivers. I can now very quickly make decisions about what assignments I will not sign up for, without any guilt or second thoughts. If I am not happy doing something, then eventually I will make those around me miserable as well.

According to *The American Time Use Survey for 2015* from the Bureau of Labor Statistics, employed Americans ages 25 to 54 with children spend an average of 8.8 hours on work-related activities. [32] Given that we spend a large percentage of our adult lives working, saying "no" to some things allows us to say "yes" to more things that are important to us. We can also apply this to extracurricular and social activities that no longer bring us joy.

- ***Stay true to you***

  Sometimes we are driven to do something to please our parents. I am sure you know of someone who entered a profession at the behest of a parent. However, if it is not aligned with your personal preferences, the result will be resentment and a lack of passion to sustain you in the long run. Sometimes we make decisions based on what our peers are doing or because we need to live up to societal expectations. That can only lead to unhappiness and regret. Of course, practical matters will have a bearing on your decisions, but to the extent that you are able, do not allow others to make decisions for you. Peer pressure and societal influences are difficult to overcome, but not if you are armed with self-knowledge and the inner fortitude to stand your ground. Instead of living by someone else's conception of who you should be, stay true to you.

- ***Consciously compromise***

  There will undoubtedly be times where we will need to make adjustments, as we rarely find a perfect fit. Do your homework. Examine the alternatives. And when you have decided upon the compromises you absolutely have to make and are willing to accept, be at peace with your decision. Move on and do not dwell on what might have been. It will drive you to distraction and the negativity will eventually consume you.

- *Follow your soul*

  If you are truly unhappy in your situation, follow your soul. Life is too short, the saying goes; this is not just a simple platitude. It may take a few days or even a few years to make a transition, but consider the downside of not making a change. Recognize that your time on this world is finite. You owe it to yourself not to be miserable for the duration. People are happiest when they are doing something that is meaningful to them. Be one of those.

- *Apply time and effort*

  Clarity and passion must be coupled with time and effort to make the progress you want towards your personal aspirations. While dreaming and visioning is important, if you don't do the work, the vision will not be attained. If you find yourself not investing towards what you want, do more soul-searching.

Doing It *With* Soul

We will naturally and effortlessly "Do It With Soul" when it is aligned with the values we consciously or subconsciously hold. But there are times when we get caught up in the processes or frameworks under which we operate. Ask whether the process is working for you or whether you are working for the process. The former cultivates, and the latter erodes our ability to "Do It With Soul."

At home

No one can argue that you are not fulfilling your role as a parent if you provide food, clothing, shelter, and education to your children. It comes from love and a sense of responsibility. Eventually, we fall into a routine and become fairly efficient in the mechanics of day-to-day living. However, like the soothing rhythm of the clickety-clack on a train, our routines can become a comfortable monotony. Or, simply satisfying our basic duties may sap our energy, leaving no room for anything else.

To "Do It With Soul" means focusing not only on the routines, but also on the essence of what binds a family together. It is more than simply going through the motions of family life. It must include the affectionate greetings, the unasked for gestures, the small kindnesses, and the shared experiences. Otherwise, we may just as well be a motley collection of strangers in a boarding house.

In fact, even if we are not that great at getting our children to school punctually every day, as long as we have trusting relationships with them, we will still have the foundation for an ongoing and emotionally rewarding family dynamic. We want them to enjoy, not dread, spending time together.

At work

Standard processes are necessary and abundant in the work environment. But the pendulum can definitely swing towards us working for the process versus the process working for us.

As an example, many consulting companies provide client organizations with a methodology that includes process frameworks and sets of tools. Ideally, the consultants are well versed in the use of the tools and/or have relevant experience in the client's industry. However, this is not always the case. To "Do It With Soul" involves tapping into experienced employees with institutional knowledge who can question, tweak, or propose a different methodology based on a clear understanding of the overall objective and of their intimate understanding of the daily operations. We cannot underestimate how much insight might be gained from those who are in the Humvees on the ground. Otherwise, we could all be marching very efficiently in the wrong direction.

Most importantly, to "Do It With Soul," involves executive leadership that promotes an open dialogue and instills trust in their employees. It involves each person coming to work daily with a sense of purpose and leaving with a sense of gratification.

"Don't gain the world and lose your soul. Wisdom is better than silver or gold."

— *Bob Marley*

Feeding the soul

Just as nutrition is vital for the body, so too is it necessary for the soul. Nourishment can be found in an elaborate vacation or a simple mindful breath of air. It can be found with a group of like-minded individuals or alone with a book. Find what feeds your soul and gorge when you can!

- *Breathe to survive*

  Pre-flight safety instructions always remind us to fit our own mask before helping anyone requiring assistance. We need to be breathing before we can do anything else. Yet we often neglect our own basic needs because we are too busy caring for others. Before we know it, we are exhausted or burnt out, or even resentful. Take care of your own immediate well-being first.

  When you take care of yourself first, you are not necessarily being selfish. Selfish is defined as concerned primarily with one's own interests, regardless of others. Putting your oxygen mask on first is very different from finishing your favorite TV program while your young child is waiting alone to be picked up from school.

- *Breathe to thrive*

  To get beyond survival, develop a daily routine of mindful breathing. Studies show that focused breathing helps to regulate our emotions and reduce stress. We can redirect our anxiety towards more productive thoughts to facilitate living a more fulfilled life. Mindfulness programs that have been introduced to organizations and schools show benefits of clearer thinking.[33]

- *Live vicariously as a supplement*

  It is conventional wisdom that one should not live vicariously. Yet it is impossible to experience first hand, everything that enhances the relatively brief time we have on this earth. Living vicariously through others is virtually (so to speak) trouble-free and there is a wide range of subject matter available to explore in the fiction and nonfiction genres. Instead of being envious of our friends' social media posts, be curious about what they are experiencing, as long as your vicarious pleasures are a supplement to, and not a replacement for, actual experiences. If you are interested in a different profession, but cannot make the leap from your current one, you can still benefit from reading related subject matter to feed your interests.

- *Savor the moment*

  Savor the moment so that you do not miss out on opportunities, both big and small, that will feed your soul. Look for the glaringly obvious and the subtle nuances. Even seemingly mundane activities can be savored, especially when you realize that what you take for granted is not accessible to someone else who may have physical or mental limitations, lack of educational opportunities, or basic human necessities.

- *Energize*

  Make a list of everyone and everything that energizes you. Spend more time with those that make you laugh or inspire you. Plan and participate in meetings or social activities that you enjoy. Seek out mentors and role models who you view as energetic. Energize others with your presence or ideas. A smile or a simple gesture of thoughtfulness can change someone's day for the better.

- *Improvise*

  Do not feel bound by stifling processes that do not adequately or appropriately serve the need. Improvise like jazz musicians do. In his book *Yes to the Mess: Surprising Leadership Lessons from Jazz*, accomplished jazz pianist and management scholar Frank Barrett says the best leaders improvise to cope with the complexity and constant changes at work. [34] Through improvisation, you become more creative and deal with situations in a real and personal way.

- *Innovate*

  Keep re-inventing yourself and try new ventures. Do not be driven purely by the desire to succeed, but by the personal growth and transformation you experience while going through the process. The outcome is never guaranteed, but you can build new skills and relationships, along with a fresh attitude.

- *Laugh*

  There is nothing like a good belly laugh to quickly lift our spirits, as long as it is not at the expense of others. Even in a professional work environment, appropriate humor reduces tension and helps to form a common bond. Laughter can transform an otherwise dull environment into a place of fun and creativity.

  "Always laugh when you can; it is cheap medicine."

  - Lord Byron

Key Principle and Action

Find your passion to actively engage

Focusing on rigid processes and on the mechanical routines of life stifles creativity and promotes mediocrity. When you exercise the freedom to tap into the essence of yourself, you can unleash dormant or hidden artistry in everything you do. And in doing so, you become more actively engaged and are more likely to find personal meaning and fulfillment. Respect yourself.

- Ask whether some of the things that you spend a lot of time doing are lifting you up or pulling you down.

- Gain clarity on what you really want in your personal and professional life.

- Take care of your basic needs first, but then live a personally enriching life.

"Don't ask yourself what the world needs; ask yourself what makes you come alive. And then go and do that. Because what the world needs is people who have come alive."

- Howard Thurman

A Final Note

"Attitude is a choice. Happiness is a choice. Optimism is a choice. Kindness is a choice. Giving is a choice. Respect is a choice. Whatever choice you make makes you. Choose wisely."
- Roy T. Bennett

Humans are social animals. We naturally seek out others and organize ourselves into groups and communities. Whether it is in our jobs or during leisure time, at work or at home, we communicate and interact with others all the time. The drive to cooperate, to share, and to partake in the journey together is the same in whichever setting we find ourselves. Who knows where the road may take us? So why not treat each other kindly along the way. Give your companions the respect they deserve, not only as individuals, but also as fellow travelers, heading for the same destination.

It is exhausting enough maintaining one persona, let alone two or more. If you treat everyone the same, whether they are family members or colleagues, beggars or kings, then you have no need to put on many different masks. How much easier is it to just be yourself?

I hope that you have found some of these principles useful. May you find joy and mutual regard at home and at work. May you choose wisely and in accordance with your inner compass. And may you always stay cool, calm, and respected.

Hello,

Thanks for reading the book!

If you have nice things to say about it, please write a review on Amazon. Feel free to also send me a note so I may thank you personally.

If you think it needs improvement, please email me. I'd love to get feedback for future revisions.

Sincerely,
Diane

diane@dianechangcoaching.com

Acknowledgments

I'd like to thank my "Cool, Calm, and Collected" family and friends who were kind enough to support and assist me in writing this book.

Words cannot express how much I appreciate your encouragement and your feedback. Your thoughtful, insightful, and honest comments were extremely valuable in helping me to improve the content and structure.

My sincere gratitude to my CG friends – Andy Scaer, David Cochran, Lesley Hanrahan, Mark Khansary, Maryann Herrera, Ric Varon, Ron Deitch, and Vicki Marshall. I knew I would get eight different perspectives based on the many helicopters and the Humvee rides we've taken together. I was not disappointed. You've always been there for me, along with many wonderful colleagues throughout the years. Thank you all.

Thank you to my coaches, Karen Sullivan and Sharon Weinreb, for your feedback. Whenever I thought I couldn't do this, your voices popped into my head as a reminder to step out of my own way.

Thank you to my illustrator, Devika Joglekar, who designed the book cover and drew the chapter illustrations. It was such a pleasure working with you.

To my sisters, Sharon Sano and Natalie King-Bhagat, my sister-in-law Caroline King, and my brothers-in-law, Amit Bhagat and Dion Chang – Thank you for your feedback and encouragement.

To my mom, Joy King and my brother, Roger King – Thanks for always being there. To my mother-in-law, Jenny Chang, and my brothers-in-law, Bart Sano and Christopher Marquard – I am blessed to have you in my life. To my extended family - having grandparents, aunts, uncles, nieces, nephews, and cousins like you has enriched my life beyond measure. And to my late dad, George King, and father-in-law, Gandy Chang – you're always here in spirit.

To Malcolm, Talisa, and Brandon – I could not have done this without you. You are my inspiration and I thank my lucky stars every day that you are in my life.

And lastly, I'd like to thank you for reading my book. I hope that you find some of the lessons I've learned helpful to you too.

With Gratitude,

Diane

About the Author

Diane Chang is a third generation Chinese South African whose career and passions have taken her around the world, from Johannesburg, to Toronto, to Chicago, to California, and now – to New York.

Diane started her career as a developer at a software consulting company in South Africa. In her early 20s, she emigrated with her family to Canada and then the United States, where she worked for six years at a global software and consulting organization. In 1995, she joined a privately held investment management organization based in Los Angeles. She worked there for 16 years until 2012, when she decided to make another big move and relocate to New York City to become an independent IT consultant and coach.

For over 20 years, Diane has delivered technology solutions in the corporate environment while managing, mentoring, and coaching individuals to develop their leadership, interpersonal, and technical skills. She's worked with executives in both business and technology to develop and implement strategic business technology roadmaps.

Diane is a Certified Professional Coach with credentials from the Institute for Professional Excellence in Coaching (iPEC) which is an International Coaching Federation (ICF) accredited program. She is certified as a Hogan Assessment consultant and as an Energy Leadership™ Index – Master Practitioner (ELI-MP). She is also a member of the ICF and participates in

Executive Coaching conferences and workshops conducted by leaders in the field.

In 2016, Diane served as the NYC Regional Network Director for Women in Technology International (WITI). Diane also mentors Africa's future via videoconference with Infinite Family, an organization that matches mentors around the world to children in South Africa who have lost one or both parents to AIDS.

Find out more:

www.dianechangcoaching.com

To book Diane to speak at your next event:

Email:

diane@dianechangcoaching.com

Connect with Diane:

LinkedIn:

https://www.linkedin.com/in/diane-chang-b0255a8/

Twitter:

https://twitter.com/dtchang

Facebook:

https://www.facebook.com/dianechangcoaching/

Instagram:

https://www.instagram.com/dianechangcoaching/

Endnotes

[1] EmpireStatofMind. "New York – Alicia Keys 'Empire State of Mind' [OFFICIAL VIDEO]." YouTube video, 4:10. Posted [23 January, 2011]. Accessed April 15, 2017. https://www.youtube.com/watch?v=oMX1sc3eOTE

[2] "About Elephant Voices; History; Joyce Poole." Elephant Voices. Accessed April 15, 2017. https://www.elephantvoices.org/about-elephantvoices/history.html

[3] Communications, Bates. "Executive Presence Assessment - ExPI™." Executive Presence Assessment (ExPI). Accessed April 15, 2017. https://www.bates-communications.com/what-we-do/executive-presence-assessment.

[4] Maxwell, John C. The 21 Indispensible Qualities of a Leader: Becoming the Person Others Will Want to Follow. Nashville, Tennessee: Thomas Nelson, 1999.

[5] Lashinsky, Adam. "Best advice I ever got. - Eric Schmidt: Hire a coach." Interview. FORTUNE. July 8, 2009. Accessed April 15, 2017.

http://archive.fortune.com/galleries/2009/fortune/0906/gallery.best_advice_i_ever_got2.fortune/14.html

Wolf Management Consultants, LLC. "Coaching - Media
Quotes." Accessed April 15, 2017.
http://www.wolfmotivation.com/programs/coaching-
media-quotes

[6] Foundation Principle used by permission of the Institute
for Professional Excellence in Coaching (iPEC)

[7] Boyatzis, Richard E., Kylie Rochford, and Scott N.
Taylor. "The role of the positive emotional attractor in
vision and shared vision: toward effective leadership,
relationships, and engagement." Frontiers. May 07, 2015.
Accessed April 15, 2017.
http://journal.frontiersin.org/article/10.3389/fpsyg.2015.00
670/full.

[8] Zak, Paul J. "The Neuroscience of Trust." Harvard
Business Review. December 19, 2016.
https://hbr.org/2017/01/the-neuroscience-of-trust.
Accessed April 15, 2017.

Covey, Stephen M.R. "How the Best Leaders Build
Trust." Leadership Now. May 2009.
http://www.leadershipnow.com/CoveyOnTrust.html.
Accessed April 15, 2017.

[9] Goleman, Daniel. Emotional intelligence: Why It Can
Matter More Than IQ. New York: Bantam Books, 2005.

[10] Glaser, Judith E. Conversational intelligence: How
Great Leaders Build Trust and Get Extraordinary Results.
Brookline, MA: Bibliomotion, Books media, 2014.

[11] Chua, Amy. *Battle Hymn of the Tiger Mother*. London: Bloomsbury, 2011.

[12] "Resilience Guide For Parents & Teachers." American Psychological Association. Accessed April 15, 2017. http://www.apa.org/helpcenter/resilience.aspx.

[13] Barragan, Rodolfo Cortes and Dweck, Carol S. "Rethinking natural altruism: Simple reciprocal interactions trigger children's benevolence." Proceedings of the National Academy of Sciences. Accessed April 15, 2017. http://www.pnas.org/content/111/48/17071.full.

[14] Richard Branson. Virgin. Accessed April 15, 2017. https://www.virgin.com/richard-branson.

[15] Jain, Naveen. "The Great Face Of Humility In An Unlikely Place." Forbes. December 24, 2012. Accessed April 15, 2017. https://www.forbes.com/sites/naveenjain/2012/12/20/richard-branson-naveen-jain-the-great-face-of-humility/#669a8c3e73cb.

[16] Official Site of Coach Wooden. Accessed April 15, 2017. http://www.coachwooden.com/.

[17] "John Wooden's favorite poems: They ask me why I teach." Millard Fillmore's Bathtub. May 06, 2015. Accessed April 15, 2017. https://timpanogos.wordpress.com/2014/02/14/john-woodens-favorite-poems-they-ask-me-why-i-teach/.

[18] Marshall Goldsmith and Mark Reiter. Triggers: Creating Behavior That Lasts – Becoming the Person You Want to Be. New York: Crown Publishing, 2015.

[19] Hogan Assessments. Accessed April 15, 2017. http://www.hoganassessments.com/ Personalysis - Wired to Thrive. Accessed April 15, 2017. http://www2.personalysis.com/. Gallup. "About StrengthsFinder 2.0." Accessed April 15, 2017. http://strengths.gallup.com/110440/About-StrengthsFinder-20.aspx.

[20] Schneider, Bruce D. Energy Leadership: Transforming Your Workplace and Your Life from the Core. Hoboken, New Jersey: John Wiley & Sons, Inc., 2008

[21] The Energy Leadership ™ Index Assessment. IPEC Energy Leadership. Accessed April 15, 2017. http://energyleadership.com/the-assessment/.

[22] "UI study finds abusive bosses don't suffer for their behavior, if they produce." University of Iowa News Services. February 4, 2010. Accessed April 15, 2017. http://news-releases.uiowa.edu/2010/february/020410abusivebosses.html.

[23] "Gratitude and Well-Being." Emmons Lab; Robert Emmons, Ph.D., Lab Director. Accessed April 15, 2017. http://emmons.faculty.ucdavis.edu/gratitude-and-well-being/.

[24] Chapman, Gary D., and Paul E. White. The 5 Languages of Appreciation in the Workplace: empowering organizations by encouraging people. Chicago. Illinois: Northfield Publishing, 2011.

[25] Foley, Mary Jo. "Microsoft does away with stack ranking." ZDNet. December 04, 2015. Accessed April 15, 2017. http://www.zdnet.com/article/microsoft-does-away-with-stack-ranking/.

[26] Eichenwald, Kurt. "Microsoft's Lost Decade." Hive. January 29, 2015. Accessed April 15, 2017. http://www.vanityfair.com/news/business/2012/08/microsoft-lost-mojo-steve-ballmer.

[27] Wood, A. M., J. J. Froh, and A. W. Geraghty. "Gratitude and well-being: a review and theoretical integration." PubMed. November 2010. Accessed April 15, 2017. https://www.ncbi.nlm.nih.gov/pubmed/20451313.

[28] Emmons, Robert A. Gratitude Works!: A 21-Day Program for Creating Emotional Prosperity. San Francisco, CA: Jossey-Bass, 2013.

[29] Holmes, Lindsay. "100 Things To Be Grateful For." The Huffington Post. November 23, 2015. Accessed April 15, 2017. http://www.huffingtonpost.com/entry/things-to-be-grateful-for-list_us_56420d6ce4b0b24aee4bcc63.

[30] Black Ivory Coffee - The World's Rarest Coffee. Accessed April 15, 2017. https://www.blackivorycoffee.com/.

[31] Gallup, Inc. "State of the American Workplace." Gallup.com. Accessed April 15, 2017. http://www.gallup.com/reports/199961/state-american-workplace-report-2017.aspx.

[32] "American Time Use Survey." U.S. Bureau of Labor Statistics. Last Modified December 20, 2016. Accessed April 15, 2017. https://www.bls.gov/tus/charts/.

[33] "Mindful Breathing." Greater Good in Action. Accessed April 15, 2017. http://ggia.berkeley.edu/practice/mindful_breathing#data-tab-how.

"Mindful at Work." Mindful. Accessed April 15, 2017. http://www.mindful.org/at-work/.

"Mindfulness for Your School, Teachers, Students." Mindful Schools. Accessed April 15, 2017. http://www.mindfulschools.org/.

[34] Barrett, Frank. *Yes to the Mess: Surprising Leadership Lessons from Jazz*. Boston, Massachusetts: Harvard Business Review Press, 2012.

46189915R00105

Made in the USA
Middletown, DE
24 July 2017